Student MIND POWER

Every Peak Has To Be Conquered

Student MIND POWER

Every Peak Has To Be Conquered

DR RANJIT KUMAR SINGH, IAS

PRABHAT
PRAKASHAN

Published by
PRABHAT PRAKASHAN PVT. LTD.
4/19 Asaf Ali Road,
New Delhi-110 002 (INDIA)
e-mail: prabhatbooks@gmail.com

ISBN 978-93-5562-409-3

STUDENT MIND POWER: EVERY PEAK HAS TO BE CONQUERED
by Dr Ranjit Kumar Singh, IAS

Edition
First, 2024

Price
₹ 400 (Rupees Four Hundred Only)

Printed at
Japan Art, Delhi

Author's Note

Welcome to the book *Student Mind Power*. This book has been specially designed to guide you in the journey to self-master your intellect. Our mind is a complex and powerful tool that can profoundly shape our lives. Even so, many of us struggle to organise our thoughts, emotions and habits. Often, we feel overwhelmed by the constant babble of our brain.

The mind is a remarkable instrument. However, if it is not organised in an effective manner, it can become a source of distress, negativity and apathy. However, the good news is that with correct knowledge, tools and practice we can learn to utilise the power of our intellect and become masters of our own intellect. The purpose of this book is to provide you with practical strategies, examples and insights that can help you control your mind and build your life in accordance with your goals, values and aspirations.

The journey to master yourself/oneself often called as 'Self Mastery' begins with self-awareness. As the ancient philosopher Socrates said, "Know thyself." The foundation of personal development and change is understanding one's thoughts, emotions and habits. In this book, we shall explore the various aspects of mind along with our ideas, emotions, beliefs, habits and perceptions. In addition to the science behind the brain, we will examine those practical instruments and techniques that can assist us in navigating our inner world with more clarity and effectiveness.

The book has been divided into many chapters, each of which is focused on a specific subject related to controlling your mind. Each chapter has been designed to make it informative, practical as well as actionable and provides you with tools and techniques that you can apply in your daily life to develop more subjectivity, flexibility, self-care and self-control. The chapters have been arranged in a logical sequence in order to prepare an extensive outline to understand and organise your mind.

In this book, you will learn about the power of your thoughts and how they shape your reality. You will learn about the role of emotions in your life and the strategy to organise them effectively. You will understand how beliefs and concepts influence your thoughts and habits. You will learn how to challenge or transform limiting beliefs. You will also learn about the habits as well as patterns of your mind and how to develop those habits that empower and strengthen you. You will discover the importance of self-care, self-acceptance and forgiveness in developing a positive intellect. You will learn strategies to make conscious decisions, be flexible in uncertain times, and increase your intellectual fitness. You will discover the art of visualisation and how it can assist in expressing your desires. You will learn strategies to develop inner peace and manage negative emotions as well. Finally, you will discover ways to increase your self-confidence and unlock your full potential.

You will find practical examples, case studies and exercises in the entire book that will help you apply these concepts in your life. These examples have been designed to explain how the strategies and techniques discussed in the book can be applied in real-life situations and how the material can be related to and applied in unique situations. You are encouraged to practice the techniques to actively engage with the material, reflect on your thoughts, emotions and habits as well as develop a deep understanding of yourself and your mind.

It is imperative to keep in mind that gaining mastery over one's intellect is a lifelong journey and for this dedication effort and practice are required. This book is not a quick solution. In fact, it is a roadmap that can guide you towards increased self-awareness, self-care and self-control. It is a tool that you can use to develop a positive mindset, cultivate healthy habits, manage your emotions, and make informed decisions. It is a resource which you can refer to, whenever you require guidance and support in the journey of mastering your mind.

I wish to express my gratitude to my mentors, teachers and all those who have inspired and directed me in my journey towards self-mastery. Their knowledge and insight have shaped my understanding of the mind and its capacity for change. I want to express my praise for the unwavering support and encouragement of my family, friends and loved ones as well, in my effort to write this book.

Readers, I am also grateful to you for choosing to begin this journey of self-mastery with me. I hope that the tools, techniques and insights provided in this book will empower you to control your mind and align your life with your true self. I encourage you to view this book with an open mind, willingness to reflect and learn as well as the commitment to practice the strategies shared in your daily life.

I believe that each person has the ability to master his own mind, develop inner peace, and build a life of fulfilment and happiness. You can transform your intellect with the correct knowledge, tools and practices and unlock your full potential. As you read the chapters of this book, I invite you to be curious, self-analytical and kind towards yourself. Please keep in mind that change takes time and hard work. It is important to be patient and kind to yourself during the journey. As you immerse yourself in the chapters of this book, you will discover practical strategies, examples and exercises that can help you develop self-awareness, regulate your views and emotions, challenge limiting beliefs, develop healthy habits, make decisions carefully, and advance yourself. You will also learn about the power of self-care, forgiveness and self-acceptance in nurturing a positive intellect and developing flexibility. The objective of the examples shared in this book is to show how strategies and techniques can be applied in real-life situations. I encourage you to actively engage with the material and reflect on your own experiences while progressing through the book.

I want to stress the fact that the journey of self-mastery is not about attaining fulfilment or eliminating all challenges in one's life. It is about you, about developing a deep understanding of your mind and emotions, and also about learning how to face the challenges of life with consciousness, resilience and knowledge. It is to recognise that you have the power to choose how you react to the circumstances in life. You can develop a positive intellect and build a life that aligns with your values and aspirations.

I hope that this book will work as a valuable resource in the journey of mastering your intellect. May this book inspire and empower you to develop inner peace, flexibility and self-confidence and lead you towards a life of purpose and happiness. Please remember that self-mastery is a lifelong journey, and it is never too late to begin.

– Dr Ranjit Kumar Singh, IAS

❑

Contents

1

Strengthening Your Intellectual Landscape

The mind is a complex landscape that all of us navigate every day. From the moment we wake up in the morning till we go to sleep at night, our thoughts and emotions shape our experience of the world. In order to become a master of your own mind, you need to learn how to navigate this landscape with skill and accuracy. In this chapter, we shall explore some practical tips and strategies to master your intellectual landscape.

Understand your thoughts

The first step in mastering your intellectual landscape is to understand your thoughts. Your thoughts are like the weather in your mind—sometimes stormy, sometimes peaceful, sometimes cloudy and sometimes clear. In order to understand your thoughts, you will have to start observing them. Focus on the thoughts that arise in your mind throughout the day. Focus on the emerging pattern and topics. Are your thoughts mostly positive or negative? Are they focused on the past, present or future? Are they useful or unhelpful?

Once you understand your thoughts, you can begin to gain control over them. You can learn to recognise unhelpful thoughts and change them with more positive and creative ones. For example, if you find yourself constantly worrying about the future, you can learn to give new form to your thoughts by focusing attention on the present moment and the things you can control now.

Practice consciousness

Consciousness is a powerful instrument to gain mastery over your intellectual landscape. It is a practice of awareness about the present moment and focusing without judgement. When you practice consciousness, you become more conscious of your thoughts, emotions and physical sensations. You learn to observe them without being involved or reacting to them.

Consciousness can help you develop peace and concentration in your mind. It can also assist in developing increased clarity and focus. By practising consciousness regularly, you can train your mind to be more present and less reactive. You will also learn to develop feelings of compassion and mercy towards yourself and others.

Create positive emotions

Emotions are a significant part of our intellectual landscape. They can shape our experience of the world and influence our behaviour. In order to master your own mind, you need to learn how to develop positive emotions. Positive emotions such as gratitude, happiness and love can help you feel happy, more content and fulfilled.

There are many ways to develop positive emotions. You can start by focusing attention on those things in your life for which you are grateful. You can also do kind deeds for yourself and others. You can engage in activities that make you happy and feel alive. By developing positive emotions, you can build a more positive intellectual landscape for yourself.

Develop self-compassion

Self-compassion is an important factor in mastering your intellectual landscape. Self-compassion is the practice of treating yourself with kindness, self-care and understanding. It involves the realisation that you are human but not perfect. It also involves being gentle with yourself when you commit mistakes or face difficult situations.

Self-compassion can help you develop increased flexibility and emotional intelligence. It can also help you develop a more positive self-image and a greater sense of self-worth. By practising self-compassion, you can learn to be more forgiving towards yourself and others. You can also develop an immense feeling of inner peace and stability.

Examples

Anita is a busy executive who often feels tensed and overwhelmed. She decided to start practising consciousness to help manage her intellectual landscape. She began to practice consciousness meditation for 10 minutes every day. During this time, she focused on her breathing and observed her thoughts and emotions without judgement. With time, she noticed that she felt calmer and more focused, even during busy and tense times at work. She also began to notice that she remained more conscious of her thoughts and feelings throughout the day and was capable of managing them in a better manner when they arose.

Johnny is a college student who struggles with anxiety and self-doubt. He decided to begin practising self-compassion to help manage his intellectual landscape. He began by writing three things for which he is grateful each day and practiced affirmation to remind himself of his worth and abilities. When he made mistakes or faced challenges, he also talked of being kind and forgiving towards himself. With time, he noticed that his level of anxiety had decreased, and he felt more confident in himself as well as his abilities.

Maria is a stay-at-home mother who frequently feels overwhelmed and tired of her daily responsibilities. She decided to begin to cultivate positive emotions to help manage her intellectual landscape. She began by preparing a list of those things that gave her happiness and satisfaction, such as spending time with her children, nature walks and reading books. She talked of participating in these activities regularly, even though it may be for a short while each day. With time, she noticed that she felt more energetic and satisfied and was capable of managing the tensions of her daily life in a better way.

Finally, mastering your intellectual landscape is a lifelong journey. For this, patience, perseverance and the desire to explore and understand your own mind are necessary. By practising consciousness, developing positive emotions and self-compassion, you can create a more positive and complete intellectual landscape for yourself. With time and practice, you can become a master of your intellect and navigate the challenges of life with more ease and simplicity.

❑

2

Harnessing Your Inner Strength

The human brain is a powerful instrument that can be used to achieve great things. However, many people fail to utilise their inner strength and ability and as a result, they live an unfulfilling life lacking in objectives. In this chapter, we will explore some practical tips and strategies to use your inner strength and unleash your full potential.

Believe in yourself

The first step in harnessing your inner power is to believe in yourself. Belief in yourself is a powerful strength that can help you overcome self-doubt and attain your goals. When you believe in yourself, you become more confident in your capabilities and more flexible in facing challenges.

To develop self-confidence, begin by focusing on your strengths and achievements. Prepare a list of those things that you are proud of and remind yourself of them regularly. Surround yourself with supportive and encouraging people who believe in you and your capabilities. Finally, be kind and gentle with yourself and avoid negative self-reflection.

Setting goals

Setting goals is a powerful way to use your inner strength and achieve your goals. Goals give you direction and objectives and help you focus on crucial issues. While setting goals, it is imperative to make them specific, measurable and attainable.

In order to set goals, start by identifying what is important to you. What are your values and priorities? What do you want to achieve in your life? Once you identify your goals, break them down into small, more manageable steps. This will help you remain inspired and focused when you work to achieve them.

Take action

Taking action is an important step in harnessing your inner power. Without action, your goals and dreams will remain no more than desires and imagination. In order to take action, you need to step out of your comfort zone and be willing to take risks.

In order to take action, identify a small step that you can take towards your goal. This can be making a phone call, sending an email, or researching something. Whatever it is, take action as soon as possible. As you take more action, you will gain more momentum and get closer to achieving your goals.

Embrace failure

Failure is a natural part of the journey towards success. Embracing failure and learning from it is a chief aspect of harnessing your inner power. When you are unsuccessful, you have an opportunity to learn from your mistakes and develop as a person. Failure also helps you develop flexibility and an intellect of development.

In order to embrace failure, begin by improving your intellect. Instead of viewing failure as a negative experience, see it as an opportunity for learning and development. Spare time to reflect on your failures and identify what you can learn from them. Finally, be kind and generous to yourself and avoid self-blame and criticism.

Examples

Sara, a recent college graduate, wanted to start her own business. She believed in herself and her potential and aimed to launch a small online store that sells handmade jewellery. She took action by researching ways of establishing an online store and purchasing supplies to make her jewellery. When she faced challenges, she embraced failure and learnt from her mistakes. With time, she built a successful business and fulfilled her dream of becoming an entrepreneur.

Moti is a middle-aged man who always dreamt of running a marathon. Despite feelings of self-doubt and fear, he aimed to run a marathon in six months. He took action by hiring a running coach and starting a training programme. When he experienced failures and injuries, he embraced failure and learnt from his mistakes. Finally, he ran the marathon and fulfilled his dream. He felt empowered and was proud of himself.

Mili is a single mother who was in a low-paid job for many years. She believed in herself and her potential. She aimed to return to school and earn a degree in nursing. She took action by researching nursing programmes and applying to schools. When she faced challenges such as maintaining a balance between work and school, she embraced failure and learnt from her mistakes. With time, she earned her degree and bagged a high-paying job as a nurse. She fulfilled her dream of earning a livelihood for her family and bringing about a change in the lives of others.

Finally, using your inner strength is an important step in achieving your goals and dreams. You can tap your full potential by believing in yourself, setting goals, taking action, embracing failure and harnessing your inner strength. With time, effort and dedication, you can achieve all that you have engaged your mind for and live a life that is fulfilling, purposeful and yours, in the true sense.

❑

3

Conquering Limiting Beliefs

Limiting beliefs are negative thoughts and beliefs that stop us from attaining our goals and living our best lives. These beliefs can be deeply entrenched and hard to eliminate. However, with the right intellect and strategies, it is possible to win them over and unlock our full potential. In this chapter, we shall explore some practical solutions and examples to win over limiting beliefs.

Identify your limiting beliefs

The first step to winning over your limiting beliefs is to recognise them. Limiting beliefs are often subconscious. Therefore, it could be helpful to spare some time to reflect on your thoughts and behaviour. Ask yourself what negative thoughts or beliefs you have about yourself or your abilities. These beliefs can be related to prior experiences, cultural or social messages or even personal insecurities.

Once you identify your limiting beliefs, write them down and consider them carefully. Ask yourself whether they are true or only negative thoughts are holding you back. It can also prove to be useful to share your beliefs with a trusted friend or physician, who can provide an objective perspective.

Challenge limiting beliefs

Once you identify your limiting beliefs, the next step is to challenge them. This involves questioning their validity and finding evidence to the contrary. For example, if you believe you are not capable enough to start your own business, then challenge this belief by searching for instances of such people, who have started successful businesses, despite facing similar challenges.

There is another way to challenge your limiting beliefs, and that is to give them a new form. Instead of seeing them as the whole truth, view them as a speculation that can be tested and proved false. This can help you change your attitude from self-doubt to curiosity and exploration.

Change limiting beliefs with positive affirmations

Apart from challenging your limiting beliefs, it is important to change them with positive affirmations. Positive affirmations are those sayings that confirm values and abilities and can help you develop a more positive and exceptional intellect.

In order to prepare positive affirmations, start by identifying those areas of your life where you struggle with limiting beliefs. Thereafter, prepare affirmations that align with your strengths and abilities in these areas. For example, if you struggle with self-doubt in your career, then say, "I am able and confident in my work, and I am valuable for my contribution."

Take action to control your limiting beliefs

Taking action to win over limiting beliefs is an important step. It is important not only to challenge and transform one's limiting beliefs but also to take concrete steps in the direction of controlling them. This can include taking risks, stepping out of one's comfort zone, and trying new things.

For example, if you have a limiting belief that you are not creative, take a class in creative endeavours such as painting or writing. This will permit you to challenge your beliefs and develop new skills and potential. The more action you take to eliminate limiting beliefs, the stronger and more self-confident you will become.

Examples

Rachit is a college student who struggles with social anxiety. He had a limiting belief that he was not interesting or charming, which prevented him from making friends and participating in social activities. He identified this belief and challenged it by reminding himself of the time when he made friends and gained positive social experiences. He changed this limiting belief with a positive affirmation: "I am interesting and worthy of being liked, and people enjoy my company." Finally, he took action by joining a social club on campus and actively participating in social programmes. With time, he achieved victory over his limiting beliefs and developed strong friendships and social relationships.

Mona, a stay-at-home mother, had a limiting belief that she was not smart enough to advance her dream of returning to school. She challenged this belief by researching programmes and speaking with consultants who helped her understand her strength and potential. She changed her limiting belief with a positive affirmation: "I am smart and capable of achieving my goals." Finally, she took action by enrolling in a part-time online programme and devoting time to studying and completing work every day. Despite facing some challenges along the way, she finally earned her degree and felt proud of her achievement. She proved to herself that she was capable of achieving anything.

David, a salesman, struggled with disapproval and had a limiting belief that he was not capable of being successful in his job. He challenged this belief by reminding himself of the time when he made successful sales and gained positive feedback from customers. He changed this limiting belief with a positive affirmation: "I am a skilled and successful salesman who provides value to my customers." Finally, he took action by taking extra training and advice from successful salespersons in his field. As he continued to take action and built his skills and self-confidence, he observed an increase in his sales and felt empowered to succeed in his job.

Finally, winning victory over limiting beliefs is an important step in mastering your mind and unlocking your full potential. By identifying and challenging negative beliefs, changing them with positive affirmations, and taking action to eliminate them, you can develop a more positive and strong intellect that enables you to achieve your goals and live your best life. Keep in mind that gaining victory over limiting beliefs is a process that takes time and effort. However, with determination and dedication you can gain control over even the most deeply entrenched beliefs and realise your full potential.

❑

4

Empowering Thoughts and Concepts

The power of our thoughts cannot be exaggerated. Our ideas shape our view of reality and influence our emotions as well as habits. If we can learn to develop empowered ideas, we can create a more positive and fulfilling life. In this chapter, we shall explore the significance of developing empowered ideas and provide examples of the same.

Identify and challenge negative thoughts

The first step in developing empowered ideas is to identify and challenge negative thoughts. Many times, we are not even aware of the negative thoughts running through our minds. Self-doubt, criticism and judgement are features of these thoughts. In order to be more conscious of these thoughts, try to focus on practising introspection inner communication. When you experience a negative thought, challenge it. Ask yourself, "Is this idea based on reality? Is it helpful or harmful? What proof do I have to support this idea?" You can begin to break the cycle of negativity by challenging negative thoughts and making way for the emergence of more empowered thoughts.

Practice gratitude

Gratitude is a powerful tool to develop empowered thoughts. When we focus on what we are grateful for, we shift our attention from negative thoughts and focus it on the positive aspects of our lives. In order to practice gratitude, spare a few minutes every day to contemplate what you are grateful for. This can be anything from the people in your life to your experiences. You can develop a more positive intellect by focusing on gratitude and attracting more positive experiences in your life.

Use positive affirmations

Positive affirmation is another powerful tool to develop empowered ideas. They are positive sayings that you repeat to develop a more positive intellect. Examples of positive affirmations include—'I am capable of achieving my goals', 'I am worthy of love and respect', and 'I am confident and flexible'. In order to use affirmations, choose one or two that resonate with you and repeat them to yourself the whole day. You can write them, say them out aloud or silently repeat them in your mind.

Surround yourself with positivity

The people and environment around us can have a significant impact on our thoughts and emotions. Surround yourself with positivity to develop positive thoughts. Spend time with those who uplift and support you and avoid those who bring you down. Surround yourself with positive affirmations and images that inspire you. Create a place that is peaceful as well as stable and that you can visit in order to reflect and recharge.

Practice consciousness

Consciousness is the practice of being present in the moment and fully occupied. By practising consciousness, we can be more aware of our thoughts and emotions and learn to control them. In order to practice consciousness, sit quietly for a few minutes every day and focus on your breathing. When your mind wanders, slowly guide it back to your breathing. As you become more skilled in consciousness, you can start applying it to other areas of your life such as food, exercising and communicating with others.

Examples

Leela, a busy professional, struggled with self-doubt and anxiety. She recognised that her negative thoughts were holding her back and decided to challenge them. When she came across a negative thought, she asked herself whether it was based on reality and whether it was helpful or harmful. She changed negative thoughts with positive affirmations, such as 'I am able and capable' and 'I trust myself to make good decisions'. She took a few minutes every day to practice consciousness to focus on her breathing and being in the present moment. As she created more empowered thoughts, she found that her anxiety decreased and she felt more self-confident in her abilities.

Paul, a college student, struggled with procrastination and self-criticism. He decided to practice gratitude by subscribing to The Daily Gratitude Journal. Every morning, he would write three things for which he was grateful, however small they may appear to be. He surrounded himself with positivity by putting up inspiring quotes and pictures in his room as well as listening to inspiring songs. When negative thoughts arose, he would challenge them by asking himself whether they were based on reality and whether they were helpful or harmful. He changed negative thoughts with positive affirmations, such as 'I am capable of achieving my goals' and 'I am worthy of success'. As he continued to develop empowered thoughts, he found that his inspiration as well as self-confidence improved, and he could control his habit of procrastination.

Sunita, a stay-at-home mother, often felt overwhelmed and tense. She decided to practice consciousness by sparing a few minutes every day to sit quietly and focus on her breathing. She surrounded herself with positivity by spending time with those friends who uplifted and supported her. When negative thoughts arose, she created a peaceful and stable environment in her home and challenged them by asking herself whether they were based on reality and whether they were helpful or harmful. She changed negative thoughts with positive affirmations, such as 'I am doing my best' and 'I am a loving and caring mother'. As she developed more empowered thoughts, she found that her stress level decreased and she could enjoy more time with her family.

Finally, developing empowered thoughts is a powerful tool to build a more positive and complete life. By identifying and challenging negative thoughts, practising gratitude, using positive affirmations, surrounding yourself with positivity, and practising consciousness, you can transform your intellectual landscape. Keep in mind that it takes time and effort to develop empowered ideas. However, with practice and perseverance, you can become a more positive intellectual and assimilate more positive experiences in your life.

❑

5

Taming the Inner Critic

The inner critic is the voice of our mind that criticises and judges our every thought, action and decision. This is the voice that tells us that we are not nice or smart or talented. The inner critic can be so powerful that it can prevent us from chasing our goals and dreams. In this chapter, we shall discuss how to tame the inner critic and remove its negative impact on our lives.

Understanding the inner critic

The inner critic is often the result of negative experiences or beliefs that we have assimilated. It can be the result of previous trauma, negative job messages or a perfectionist intellect. The inner critic can be helpful at times. It inspires us to strive for excellence and avoid mistakes. However, when it becomes unceasing and extremely critical, it can be the reason for self-doubt, anxiety and depression.

Taming the inner critic

Recognise the voice of your inner critic—the first step in controlling one's inner critic is to be conscious of its presence. Identify when it becomes discernible and what it says. Once you identify the voice of your inner critic, you can start challenging its negative messages.

Challenge the inner critic—When the inner critic starts criticising you, challenge it by asking yourself if its criticism is based on reality. Often, the criticism of the inner critic is based on illogical fears or beliefs. Ask yourself if what the inner critic is saying is true or if it is only a negative thought.

Change negative self-discussion with positive affirmations—Instead of listening to the negative messages of your inner critic, change them with positive affirmations. Affirmations can be simple sayings, such as 'I am worthy of love and respect', or 'I am capable of attaining my goals'. These affirmations can help in redressing the negative self-discussion of the inner critic.

Practice self-compassion—Be kind to yourself and treat yourself with the same kindness and compassion that you would show any friend. Keep in mind that everyone makes mistakes and has flaws. Accept yourself for who you are and focus on your virtues instead of your weaknesses.

Examples

Som, a graphic designer, often struggled with the voice of his inner critic. He constantly found himself criticising his work and worrying that it was not good enough. In order to tame his inner critic, Som started identifying when it became discernible and challenged its negative messages. When his inner critic said that his work was not good enough, Som asked himself whether it was based on reality. He changed negative self-discussion with positive affirmations, such as 'I am a talented graphic designer' and 'My work deserves recognition'. As he practiced controlling his inner critic, he found that his self-confidence improved and he was more willing to take creative risks.

Radhika, a student, often struggled with the voice of the inner critic while talking about her grades. She found herself constantly worrying that she would fail and was not very smart. In order to tame her inner critic, Radhika started identifying when it became discernible and challenged its negative messages. When the inner critic said that she was not sufficiently intelligent, Radhika asked herself whether it was based on reality. She changed negative self-discussion with positive affirmations, such as, 'I am a hardworking student' and 'I am capable of earning a good grade'. As she practiced controlling her inner critic, she found that the level of her anxiety had decreased and she could focus more on her studies.

Finally, our inner critic can be a powerful force in our lives, but it is possible to control it and eliminate its negative impact. We can learn to be masters of our own minds by identifying the voice of the inner critic, challenging its negative messages, changing negative self-discussion with positive affirmations, and practising self-compassion. It takes time and practice to control the inner critic, but with determination, we can learn to live a more positive and fulfilling life. Keep in mind that self-doubt and negative self-discussion are normal experiences. If necessary, it is advisable to seek the help of a doctor or consultant. By taking a step to control the inner critic, we can create a more empowered and self-affirming inner dialogue, which will help us reach our full potential.

❑

6

Developing Intellectual Flexibility

Intellectual flexibility is the ability to adapt to adverse circumstances and back away. It is the ability to recover from tensions, shocks and jolts. It is important to build intellectual flexibility to maintain good mental health and achieve success in life. In this chapter, we shall discuss building intellectual flexibility and strategies to overcome challenges.

Understanding intellectual flexibility

Intellectual flexibility is not about being immune to stress or difficulties. Instead, it is about developing the necessary skills and resources required to deal with adverse circumstances. Intellectual flexibility is built through a combination of factors including a positive outlook, social support, emotional regulation and problem-solving skills.

Building intellectual flexibility

Develop an intellect for growth—This is the belief that your abilities and skills can be developed through hard work and dedication. It is opposed to a decided (hard and fast) intellect which is a belief that your abilities are written in stone. You can overcome obstacles and failures more easily by evolving an intellect for growth.

Build social support—Social support is a crucial component of intellectual resilience. It is important to have a network of friends, family and colleagues, who can provide emotional support and practical help, whenever required. Building strong ties and maintaining social relationships can help you deal with stress and adversity.

Practice consciousness—Consciousness is the practice of being in the present and focusing on one's thoughts and emotions without decision. By practising consciousness, you can develop more self-awareness, emotional regulation and resilience. Consciousness can also help you manage stress and anxiety.

Take care of your physical health—Physical health has a deep connection with mental well-being. A healthy diet, regular exercise and sufficient sleep can help you build intellectual resilience and deal with stress.

Develop problem-solving skills—Learning to solve problems effectively is an important part of building intellectual resilience. By developing problem-solving skills, you can face challenges with a positive outlook and find creative solutions for adverse circumstances.

Examples

Esha, a college student, often struggled to balance her part-time job with her academic workload. She would feel overwhelmed and tense and was at a loss so as to understand how to manage her time effectively. To build her intellectual resilience, Esha started by developing an intellect for growth. She reminded herself that she could overcome this challenge by working hard and focusing attention. She enlisted the support of her friends and family as well and began to practice consciousness, in order to manage her stress level. She also took care of her physical health by consuming healthy food, exercising regularly and sleeping for a sufficient time. She also developed problem-solving skills by breaking down her workload into manageable parts and preparing a schedule, which permitted her to balance her responsibilities effectively. As Esha built her intellectual flexibility, she began to develop problem-solving skills and felt more positive.

David, the owner of a small business, fought to save his business during the Covid-19 pandemic. He felt stressed and worried about the future of his business. David began to evolve an intellect for growth to build intellectual resilience. He reminded himself that he had the necessary skills and resources to adapt to the current situation. He also consulted his colleagues and peers for support and advice. David practiced awareness to manage the level of his stress, and by exercising regularly and consuming healthy food, took care of his physical health. He also developed problem-solving skills by finding creative solution of researching new strategies to run his business and save it during a pandemic. As David built intellectual resilience, he developed the necessary skills and resources to deal with stress and overcome failures.

Finally, in order to maintain good intellectual health and gain success in life, it is necessary to build intellectual flexibility. By evolving an intellect for development, building social support, practising consciousness, taking care of your physical health, and developing problem-solving skills, you can overcome challenges and avoid adversity. Intellectual flexibility is not something that can be developed overnight. However, with constant effort and practice, the necessary skills and resources can be built to deal with any stress and overcome failures.

Keep in mind that intellectual flexibility is not about being complete in yourself or never experiencing any difficulty. It is about adapting to change, managing stress, and being capable of overcoming challenges. By building intellectual flexibility, you can improve your overall well-being and achieve success in all areas of your life.

❑

7

Adopting Positive Self-dialogue

Our inner dialogue, which is also known as self-discussion, has a significant impact on our mental health and well-being. How we speak to ourselves can either empower or break us. Unfortunately, many people are engaged in negative self-dialogue without being aware of it, which can lead to self-doubt, low self-esteem and anxiety. However, by adopting positive self-dialogue, we can transform our intellect and build a more positive and fulfilling life.

What is positive self-discussion?

Positive self-discussion is the practice of using encouraging, positive and supportive language while talking to yourself. This includes changing negative thoughts with positive ones and changing our inner self-dialogue in such a way that it supports our goals and values. Positive self-discussion is not about ignoring reality or portraying that all is well. It is about dealing with circumstances with an intellect for development and focusing on the positive aspects of a situation, instead of negative ones.

Examples of positive self-discussion

Some examples of positive self-discussion are given here, which you can use to transform your intellect and increase your self-confidence:

"I am capable of managing this situation."
"I am strong and resilient."
"I am worthy of love and respect."
"I am proud of my accomplishments."
"I am progressing towards my goals."
"I am grateful for the blessings in my life."
"I trust my ability to overcome any obstacle."
"I choose to focus on the positive aspects of this situation."
"I deserve happiness and success."
"I am enough, just the way I am."

Advantages of positive self-discussion

There are many advantages of practising positive self-dialogue. Some methods are given here, which if adopted in positive self-discussion, can improve your intellectual health and well-being.

Increases self-confidence—By changing negative self-dialogue with positive affirmations, you can increase your self-confidence and improve your self-esteem.

Reduces anxiety—Negative self-dialogue can be a chief source of anxiety. By changing negative thoughts with positive ones, you can reduce your anxieties and improve your overall sense of well-being.

Improvement in flexibility—Positive self-dialogue can help you avoid failures and overcome challenges. You can create a feeling of flexibility and adaptability by viewing situations in a positive light.

Increases inspiration—Positive self-dialogue can help you remain inspired and focused on your goals. By using enthusiastic language, you can remain energetic and committed to achieving your goals.

Improves relationships—Positive self-dialogue can help you communicate more effectively and establish better relationships. By facing situations with a positive intellect, you can improve your conversations with others and develop more positive relationships.

Tips to adopt positive self-dialogue

Some tips are given below to adopt positive self-dialogue:

Practice self-awareness—Pay attention to your inner dialogue. Pay attention when you are engaged in negative self-dialogue.

Challenge negative thoughts—When you notice negative self-dialogue, challenge it by asking yourself whether it is true and if there is proof to support it.

Reframe negative thoughts—Once you recognise negative thoughts, frame them once again in a positive form. For example, instead of saying, "I am not good enough," say, "I am enough just the way I am."

Use positive quotes— Use positive quotes to remember your strengths and abilities. Repeat them to yourself the whole day, especially when you are feeling sad or frustrated.

Surround yourself with positivity—Surround yourself with positive people, positive media, and positive experiences. This will help in strengthening positive self-dialogue and developing a more positive intellect.

Finally, adopting positive self-dialogue can have a profound impact on our intellectual health and well-being. By changing negative thoughts with positive ones and reframing our inner dialogue, we can increase our self-confidence, reduce anxiety, and improve our flexibility. Effort and self-awareness are required to practice positive self-dialogue. With time and practice, you can develop a more positive intellect and build a more fulfilling life.

❑

8

Navigating Your Inner World

The human brain is a vast and complex landscape. There are a multitude of ideas, emotions and beliefs within it, each vying for attention and dominance. Navigating this inner world can be a daunting task, but it is necessary if we want to become masters of our intellect. In this chapter, we shall explore some practical strategies to navigate your inner world and present examples of how they can be applied in daily life.

Consciousness

Consciousness is the practice of bringing your focus to the present moment, without judgement or distraction. It is a powerful tool to navigate your inner world because it permits you to observe your thoughts and sentiments without them being swept away. When you practice awareness, you become more conscious about your intellectual processes and can begin to recognise those patterns and triggers that can be the cause of negative thoughts or sentiments.

For example, let us assume that you are at work and receive an email from your boss that is important for your current work. Your initial reaction can be of anger or defensiveness. However, if you practice consciousness, you can perceive these emotions without being trapped in them. You can see whether your anger is rooted in the fear of failure or if your defensiveness is the result of feeling undervalued. By recognising these inherent emotions, you can start addressing them in more creative ways.

Journaling

Journaling is another powerful tool to navigate one's inner world. By putting down your thoughts and emotions on paper, you can gain a better understanding of your intellectual processes and recognise those patterns that can be the cause of negative thoughts or emotions. Journaling can help you work through difficult emotions as well as arrive at solutions for problems.

For example, let us assume that you are struggling with anxiety. By journaling about your worried thoughts and emotions, you can start identifying those triggers that become the cause of your anxiety. You can also come up with strategies that can help you manage your anxieties more effectively.

Self-reflection

Self-reflection is the practice of examining your own thoughts, emotions and behaviour. This can help you identify those areas where you can get trapped or may need to bring about changes in order to achieve your objectives. Self-reflection can also help you develop self-awareness and a feeling of sympathy towards others.

For example, let us assume that you are facing difficulties in your personal relationships. By reflecting upon your own thoughts, feelings and behaviour, you can start recognising those patterns that are causing conflict. You can also gain a better understanding of your own emotional requirements and also learn how they are affecting your relationships.

Cognitive restructuring

Cognitive restructuring is a technique that is used in cognitive behaviour therapy to help people recognise and change negative thought patterns. This involves recognising negative thoughts and changing them with more positive and creative ones. Cognitive restructuring can be a powerful tool to navigate your inner world because it can help in liberating you from negative thought patterns that can hold you back.

For example, let us assume that you catastrophise situations. You can automatically assume the worst scenario in any situation. By practising cognitive restructuring, you can learn to recognise these negative thought patterns and change them with more realistic and creative thoughts. You can start perceiving situations in a more balanced way, which can lead to more flexibility and improvement in intellectual health.

Emotional regulation

Emotional regulation is the ability to manage your emotions in a healthy and creative manner. This not only involves recognising and accepting your emotions, but also, being capable of controlling their intensity and duration. Emotional regulation can be a powerful tool to navigate your inner world because it can help you manage difficult emotions and avoid being overwhelmed by them.

For example, let us assume that you are feeling overwhelmed by stress. By practising emotional regulation techniques such as deep breathing or consciousness, you can start controlling your emotions and prevent them from becoming out of control. You can also develop strategies to cope with them that can help you manage stress more effectively, such as taking breaks throughout the day or participating in physical activities.

Seeking support

Navigating one's inner world can be a challenging process and it is important to remember that you do not have to do this alone. Seeking support from friends, family members or intellectual health professionals can be a powerful tool for managing your thoughts, emotions and beliefs.

For example, let us assume that you are struggling with depression. By asking for help from a doctor, you can become capable of identifying underlying issues that are contributing to your depression and develop a treatment plan that can help you manage your symptoms. You can also benefit from help groups or peer counselling, where you can connect with other people who are going through similar experiences.

Mindful movement

Mindful movement is a practice that links physical movement with consciousness. This involves bringing your focus to your body and activities, without judgement or distraction. Mindful movement can be a powerful tool for navigating your inner world because it can help you connect with your body and remove physical stress which can contribute to negative thoughts or emotions.

For example, let us assume that you are feeling anxious. By practising mindful movements such as yoga or Tai chi, you can begin to liberate yourself from physical stress and connect with your breathing. You may also find that mindful movement helps you feel more grounded and present in the moment, which in turn, can help reduce anxiety.

Taking care of yourself

Self-care is the practice of taking care of your physical, intellectual and emotional welfare. This involves being engaged in activities that boost health and welfare, such as exercise, nutritious food and relaxation techniques. Self-care can be a powerful tool for navigating your inner world because it can help you reduce stress and boost overall well-being.

For example, let us assume that you are feeling overwhelmed with work. By engaging in self-care activities such as walking or taking a warm bath, you can start reducing stress and boost relaxation. You can also benefit from those activities that boost intellectual and emotional welfare, such as meditation.

Finally, navigating one's inner world is a lifelong process but it may bring special rewards. By practising consciousness, journaling, self-reflection, cognitive restructuring, emotional regulation, seeking support, mindful movement and self-care, you can develop a broad understanding of self-awareness and learn to manage your thoughts, emotions and beliefs in a healthy and creative manner. These strategies can be applied to all areas of life from personal relationships and work to overall welfare. With practice and determination, you can become a master of your own intellect and navigate your inner world with more ease and clarity.

❑

9

Unlocking Intellectual Potential

Unlocking your intellectual potential is about harnessing the full range of your cognitive abilities, including memory, creativity, problem-solving and critical thinking. By optimising the performance of your brain, you can increase the overall quality of your life and achieve your goals with more ease and efficiency.

In this chapter, we shall explore some major strategies to unlock your intellectual potential.

Mental exercises

Just as physical exercise is necessary for your body to remain healthy, your brain requires intellectual exercise in order to remain sharp. Mental exercises can help you improve your memory, focus and overall cognitive functions.

For example, you can try playing brain games such as crossword puzzles, Sudoku or brain teasers. You can also participate in those activities that challenge your brain, such as learning a new language, playing a musical instrument, or adopting a new hobby. By regularly participating in these activities, you can strengthen your nervous system and improve the performance of your brain.

Meditation

Meditation is a practice that involves focusing on the current moment without judgement or distraction. It has been shown to have many benefits for intellectual health, including reducing stress and anxiety, improving focus, and increasing creativity.

For example, you can try consciousness meditation which involves focusing on your breathing and thoughts without judgement. By practising consciousness regularly, you can train your mind to focus more effectively as well as manage your thoughts and emotions more skilfully.

Sleep

Sleep is necessary for optimal brain activity. When you sleep, your brain consolidates memories and clears toxic substances that can accumulate during waking hours. It is essential to get sufficient high-quality sleep for cognitive performance, memory, creativity and problem-solving.

For example, you can try to establish a routine of consistent sleep by sleeping and waking at the same time every day. You can also create a sleep-friendly environment by keeping your bedroom cool, dark and peaceful.

Nutrition

Your brain needs nutrients in order to work properly. A nutritious diet that includes food such as fruits, vegetables, whole grains and lean protein can help you optimise the performance of your brain.

For example, you can try to include more brain-healthy food products in your diet, such as leafy vegetables, black plums (jamun), nuts and fish. You can also avoid processed foods, sugary drinks and alcohol which can harm cognitive functions.

Learning

Learning is a critical component to unlocking your intellectual potential. By constantly exploring new knowledge and skills, you can challenge your brain and expand your cognitive abilities.

For example, you can participate in new programmes, workshops or conferences, or read books on a wide range of subjects. You can stimulate your brain by exposing yourself to new ideas and concepts as well as enhance your creativity and problem-solving skills.

Visualisation

Visualisation is a powerful tool to unlock your intellectual potential. This involves creating mental images of the results that you want to achieve. This can help you focus your attention and inspiration.

For example, you can try to imagine achieving your goals, such as completing a project or winning a competition. By creating a clear mental image of success, you can increase your inspiration and focus on achieving your goals.

Setting goals

Setting objectives is another important strategy in order to unlock your intellectual potential. By setting clear and attainable goals, you can focus your attention and inspiration on specific results.

For example, you can set short-term and long-term objectives in different areas of your life, such as career, relationships, health and personal development. By breaking down your goals into small, attainable steps, you can create a feeling of progress and motion, which can help you remain inspired and on track.

Positive thinking

Positive thinking is a powerful tool to unlock your intellectual potential. By developing a positive intellect, you can improve your mental health and enhance your overall cognitive functions.

For example, by focusing attention on your strengths and achievements as well as practising gratitude for the positive aspects of your life, you can try to transform negative thoughts into positive ones. By developing a positive intellect, you can reduce stress and anxiety, improve your mood, and enhance cognitive abilities.

Consciousness

Consciousness is another important strategy to unlock your intellectual potential. It involves being present in this moment without judgement or distraction and can help in improving focus, reducing stress and increasing creativity.

For example, you can try focusing on breathing, or the subtle movements of the body, or practice walking. By practising consciousness regularly, you can train your mind to focus more effectively, manage your thoughts and emotions more skillfully, and enhance your overall cognitive functions.

Exercise

Exercise is not only beneficial to your physical health but also, to intellectual health and cognitive functions. Regular exercise can help to reduce stress and anxiety, improve mood, and enhance cognitive functions.

For example, you can try to include regular physical activities in your routine, such as walking, running, swimming or cycling. By engaging in regular physical activities, you can improve your overall health and well-being as well as enhance your cognitive abilities.

Conclusion

An overall perspective is required in order to unlock your intellectual potential. This involves optimising brain performance through many strategies such as mental exercises, meditation, sleep, nutrition, learning, visualisation, setting goals, positive outlook, consciousness and exercise. By including these strategies in your routine, you can enhance your cognitive abilities, improve your intellectual health, and achieve your goals with more ease and efficiency.

❑

10

Developing Self-consciousness

Self-consciousness is an integral component of personal development and growth. This is the ability to recognise your own emotions, thoughts as well as behaviour and understand how they affect your life and relationships. It is essential to develop self-consciousness in order to gain success, build healthy relationships, and live a full life. In this chapter, we shall explore some practical ways to develop self-consciousness.

Journaling

Journaling is an effective instrument to develop self-consciousness. Writing down your thoughts and emotions can help you learn about your own inspirations and behaviour. By considering your journal entries, you can recognise those patterns and subjects that are affecting your life.

For example, you can try writing in your diary every day or whenever you feel the need to reflect on your thoughts and emotions. By regularly participating in this exercise, you can develop more self-consciousness and gain a deeper understanding of yourself.

Consciousness meditation

Consciousness meditation is another powerful tool for developing self-consciousness. It involves focusing on the current moment without judgement or distraction and can help you become more aware of your thoughts, emotions and physical sensations.

For example, you can practice consciousness meditation for a few minutes every day. By focusing on your breathing and being in the present, you can develop more self-consciousness and improve your overall well-being.

Self-reflection

Self-reflection is an important exercise to develop self-consciousness. It involves taking some time out to reflect upon your thoughts, emotions as well as behaviour and consider how they are affecting your life.

For example, you can try taking some time every week to reflect upon your life and relationships. By regularly engaging in self-reflection, you can gain a deep understanding of yourself and develop more self-consciousness.

Emotional intelligence

Emotional intelligence is the ability to recognise and manage your emotions as well as those of others. The development of emotional intelligence is essential in order to establish healthy relationships and achieve success in life.

For example, you can try to work on your emotional intelligence by being more conscious of how your emotions affect your behaviour. By practising sympathy and understanding the emotions of others, you can improve interpersonal skills and develop more self-consciousness.

Personality tests

Personality tests can be a useful instrument to develop self-consciousness. Along with your strengths and weaknesses, it can provide information about your personality traits and tendencies.

For example, you can try taking personality tests such as the Myers-Briggs Type Indicator (MBTI) or Big Five Personality traits tests. By understanding your personality type, you can gain more self-awareness and insight into your own behaviour.

Seek feedback

Taking feedback from others can also be a useful instrument to develop self-consciousness. Asking others for their honest opinion and viewpoints can provide insight into how they feel about you.

For example, you can try asking your trusted friends or colleagues for their feedback on your behaviour or performance. You can gain a fresh perspective about yourself by considering their input and developing more self-consciousness.

Practice active listening

Active listening is an important skill in order to develop self-consciousness. It involves listening to others with an open mind and paying attention to their ideas and emotions.

For example, you can practice active listening by paying attention to the ideas and emotions of others during a conversation. By developing this skill, you can be more conscious of your own communication style and improve your relationship with others.

Recognise your triggers

Identifying your triggers is an important step in developing self-consciousness. Triggers are situations or incidents that cause you to react emotionally and can provide insight into your own behaviour and thought patterns.

For example, you can try to identify your triggers by paying attention to those situations or incidents that inspire you to react emotionally. By being more conscious of your triggers, you can develop strategies to manage your emotions and improve your overall well-being.

Practice self-compassion

The practice of self-compassion is another significant aspect of developing self-consciousness. It involves treating yourself with compassion as well as understanding and recognising that everyone makes mistakes.

For example, when you make a mistake or experience failure, you can try to practice self-compassion by being kind to yourself. By developing this skill, you can improve your self-esteem and develop more self-consciousness.

Reflect on your values

Reflecting on your values is an important step in developing self-consciousness. Your values are your principles and beliefs that guide your behaviour and decisions.

For example, you can try to reflect upon your values by focusing on what is most important for you in life. By identifying your values, you can gain more understanding of your objectives as well as direction and develop more self-consciousness.

Finally, developing self-consciousness is an important component of personal growth and development. By practising journaling, consciousness meditation, self-reflection, emotional intelligence, seeking feedback, active listening, identifying triggers, practising self-compassion, and reflecting upon your values, you can gain more insight into your thoughts, emotions and behaviour. Develop a greater sense of self-awareness. By becoming more self-conscious, you can improve your relationships, gain success in life, and live a more complete and meaningful life.

❑

11

Controlling Negative Thinking

Negative thinking can be a big obstacle to living a happy and prosperous life. When you constantly think negatively, it can affect your mood, relationships and even your physical well-being. However, the good news is that with practice and effort, you can control negative thinking and develop a more positive outlook on life.

Recognise negative thoughts

The first step in controlling negative thinking is to be aware of your negative thoughts. Negative thoughts can be automatic and sometimes, no one notices them. Therefore, it is important to pay attention to your inner dialogue.

For example, if you constantly find yourself thinking that you are not good enough, try to recognise those situations or triggers that give rise to this idea. By being more conscious of your negative thoughts, you can start challenging them and develop a more positive outlook.

Challenge negative thoughts

Once you identify your negative thoughts, the next step is to challenge them. Negative thoughts are often illogical and can be based on faulty ideas or beliefs. By challenging these negative thoughts, you can liberate yourself from the cycle of negativity and develop a more positive outlook.

For example, if you have a negative thought, such as 'I am not good enough?' try to challenge it by asking yourself whether it is true. Are there any examples in your life where you have been successful or done well? By questioning your negative thoughts, you will realise that they are frequently based on baseless beliefs.

Redefine negative thoughts

Redefining negative thoughts involves looking at a situation from a fresh perspective. By changing your way of thinking about any situation, you can start looking at its positive aspects and develop a more positive outlook.

For example, if you have a negative thought, such as 'I always fail', try to reframe it by looking at the positive aspects of your failures. What did you learn from your failures? How did they help you grow and develop? By redefining your negative thoughts, you can start looking at the positive aspects of your experiences.

Practice gratitude

Practising gratitude is another way of controlling negative thinking. When you focus on what you are grateful for, it can help you remove your focus from negative thoughts and develop a more positive outlook.

For example, try to form the habit of listing three things for which you are grateful every day. These can be simple things such as a beautiful sunset or a kind gesture from a friend. By focusing on the positive aspects of your life, you can start realising that there is much for which you can be grateful.

Be with positive people

The people whom you surround yourself with can also have an effect on your thinking. Surrounding yourself with positive and supportive people can help you develop a more positive outlook and eliminate negative thinking.

For example, try to spend more time with those who uplift you and make you feel good about yourself. Distance yourself from such people who are negative or demeaning you. By surrounding yourself with positive people, you can start seeing the good in the world around you.

Practice self-care

Practising self-care is another important aspect of controlling negative thinking. When you give priority to your physical and emotional well-being, you can develop a more positive outlook and control negative thinking.

For example, try cultivating the habits of getting sufficient sleep, consuming healthy food, and exercising regularly. Practice activities of self-care such as taking bubble baths, going for a walk amidst nature, or listening to your favourite song. By prioritising self-care, you can improve your mood and develop a more positive outlook.

Practice consciousness

Consciousness is a powerful instrument to control negative thinking. When you practice consciousness, you learn to observe your thoughts and emotions without judgement. This can help liberate you from the pattern of negative thinking and develop a more positive outlook.

For example, try to practice consciousness meditation for a few minutes every day. Concentrate on your breathing and observe your thoughts without judgement. When negative thoughts arise, accept them and let them go. By practising consciousness, you can develop a sense of self-consciousness and control your thoughts.

Seek professional help

If you are struggling to overcome negative thoughts on your own, do not hesitate to seek professional help. An intellectual health professional can help you develop strategies to control negative thinking and provide you with assistance and guidance along the way.

For example, Cognitive Behaviour Therapy (CBT) is a type of treatment that is focused on recognising and challenging negative thoughts. A doctor can work with you to recognise your negative thoughts and help you develop strategies to challenge as well as redefine them.

Finally, negative thinking can be a big obstacle to living a happy and prosperous life. However, with practice and effort, you can control negative thinking and develop a more positive outlook. By recognising and challenging your negative thoughts and developing positive habits such as gratitude, self-care and consciousness, you can control your thoughts and live a more fulfilling life. If you are struggling to overcome negative thoughts on your own, do not hesitate to seek professional help. Remember, you are capable of controlling negative thinking as well as living a happy and fulfilling life.

❑

12

Developing a Strong Intellect

A strong intellect is an important element to achieve success in any area of life. They are the perspectives, beliefs and ideas that we hold in our mind. They decide how we observe situations and react to them. A strong intellect gives us the strength to rise from challenges and failures, focus attention, remain inspired, and achieve our goals. In this chapter, we shall explore the importance of developing a strong intellect and provide examples of how you can develop and strengthen your own intellect.

Believe in yourself

Believing in yourself is among the most important aspects of creating a strong intellect. When you believe in yourself, you develop the self-confidence and courage to face new challenges and pursue your goals. On the other hand, if you lack confidence in yourself, you can hesitate, doubt your abilities, and accept defeat easily. Therefore, to develop a strong intellect, it is essential to create self-confidence.

In order to create self-confidence, focus on your strengths and achievements instead of your weaknesses and failures. Reflect upon that time when you faced challenges and were successful.

Surround yourself with helpful people who encourage and believe in you. Keep in mind that everyone has weaknesses but you can overcome them and gain success.

Embrace challenges

Accepting challenges is another important aspect of creating a strong intellect. Challenges can be difficult and scary but they also provide an opportunity to learn, grow and develop flexibility. When you face challenges with an intellect for growth, you see them as an opportunity to overcome obstacles instead of avoiding them.

For example, if you are scared of public speaking, you can see this as an opportunity to develop your communication skills and control your fear. Instead of avoiding occasions of public speaking, search them out and focus on improving your skills every time. This outlook will help you create self-confidence and develop a strong intellect.

Focus on solutions, not problems

Problems can be resolved in a better way by focusing on solutions instead of problems. When you face obstacles or failures, it is easy to get trapped in focusing on problems and negative thinking. However, a strong intellect faces problems as an opportunity to explore solutions.

Focus on what you can control instead of what you cannot, in order to develop this intellect. Identify the problem and then, brainstorm possible solutions. Evaluate each solution and choose the one that is most likely to work. This outlook will help you develop an active intelligence and avoid feeling helpless in facing challenges.

Build flexibility

Flexibility is the ability to bounce back from failures and challenges. It is an important element of a strong intellect because it enables you to remain determined and maintain focus in unfavourable circumstances. In order to develop resilience, consider the following methods:

Develop a positive intellect—Create optimism and focus attention on the positive aspects of life.

Practice self-care—Take care of your physical, emotional and intellectual health by exercising regularly, getting sufficient sleep, and participating in activities that make you happy.

Create a support system—Surround yourself with helpful people who encourage and believe in you.

Embrace failure—Look at failure as an opportunity to learn and grow instead of a personal fault or weakness.

Be willing—Be ready to adjust your perspective and try new strategies when faced with obstacles or failures.

Practice gratitude

Gratitude is the practice of focusing on the positive aspects of life and being grateful for whatever we have in life. This is an essential element of a strong intellect because it helps us maintain perspective and appreciate the good things in life, even during difficult times.

In order to practice gratitude, start a daily gratitude journal or spare a few minutes every day and reflect upon what you are grateful for. Pay attention to small things in life, such as a beautiful sunset, a kind word from a friend, or a hot cup of tea. By practising gratitude regularly, you will gain help in developing a more optimistic outlook on life, which is an essential component of a strong intellect.

Set goals and take action

By setting goals and initiating action to achieve them, it becomes easy to attain them. Goals give us direction as well as objectives and help us focus on our energy and resources. When we take action towards achieving our goals, we create momentum as well as the feeling of progress and achievement.

In order to set effective goals, they should be specific, measurable and attainable. Divide big goals into small, manageable stages and set a deadline for each one. Take consistent action towards your goals, even if they are only small steps. This approach will help you build momentum and move forward in the direction of achieving your goals.

Learn from failure

Finally, the specialty of a strong intellect is the desire to learn from failure. Failure is an inevitable part of life, but how do we react to failure? This decides the level of our success. When we face failure with an intellect for development, we see it as an opportunity for learning and improvement instead of personal fault or weakness.

In order to learn from failure, think about what went wrong and identify what you could have done differently. Use this information to adjust your perspective and try again. Failure is a natural part of the process of learning, and it is important to embrace it to develop a strong intellect and as an opportunity to develop the same.

Finally, building a strong intellect is a continuous process, for which conscious effort and practice are required. By believing in yourself, accepting challenges, focusing on solutions, cultivating flexibility, practising gratitude, setting goals, taking action, and learning from failure, you can develop an intellect that empowers you to overcome obstacles, achieve your goals and live a fulfilling life. Remember, a strong intellect is not about being perfect or having all the answers; it is about having the courage and resilience to face challenges and move forward constantly.

❑

13

Managing Stress and Anxiety

Stress and anxiety are normal experiences that affect our intellectual and physical health. When left unchecked, they can lead to many negative results, including depression, insomnia and chronic health conditions. However, by learning effective strategies to manage stress and anxiety, we can improve our well-being and quality of life. In this chapter, we shall explore a few effective techniques to manage stress and anxiety.

Recognise triggers

The first step in managing stress and anxiety is to recognise what triggers these emotions. Triggers can be internal, such as negative thoughts or physical problems, or external, such as stressful situations or relationships. By understanding the reasons that trigger our stress and anxiety, we can develop strategies to manage them.

An effective way to identify triggers is to maintain a journal or log of our thoughts and emotions for the entire day. This can help us recognise patterns and triggers about which we may be unaware.

Practice consciousness

Consciousness is a technique that includes focusing on the present moment without judgement. Bringing our focus to the present moment instead of ruminating about the past or worrying about the future can help reduce stress and anxiety.

There are many ways of practising consciousness. These include meditation, yoga and deep breathing exercises. Taking a few deep breaths while focusing on the sensation of the flow of air inside and outside the body is an easy consciousness exercise. As soon as your thoughts or concentration are disturbed, accept them and lead your focus back to your breathing.

Exercise regularly

Exercise is a natural stress deterrent that can help reduce anxiety as well. Physical activity releases endorphins which are natural mood booster hormones and can help improve our overall sense of well-being. Regular exercise can also help us build resilience towards stress by increasing our physical as well as emotional strength. Taking a short walk or a few minutes of stretching can also help to reduce stress and anxiety.

Practice relaxation techniques

Relaxation techniques such as muscle relaxation and guided imagery can help to reduce stress and anxiety by enhancing the sensation of calmness and rest. These techniques involve the deliberate stretching and releasing of different groups of muscles in the body or imagining peaceful images (scenes) and sensations.

Setting boundaries

Setting boundaries is an indispensable part of managing stress and anxiety. Boundaries can help us maintain healthy relationships and stop us from taking on more than we can manage. This can include setting the limit of our working hours, saying no to commitments that do not conform with our priorities, and setting clear expectations of our needs and boundaries with others.

Seek support

Talking with a trusted friend or family member, or seeking professional help from a doctor or consultant can also help in managing stress and anxiety. By talking about our feelings, we can get help in processing them and gaining perspective on our challenges. An intellectual health professional can also provide guidance and help in order to develop effective coping strategies.

Finally, the management of stress and anxiety is a continuous process that requires conscious effort and practice. By identifying triggers, practising consciousness, exercising regularly, using relaxation techniques, setting boundaries, and seeking help, we can improve our well-being and reduce the effect of stress and anxiety on our life. Remember, it is important to prioritise your intellectual health and look after yourself, even in challenging circumstances.

❑

14

Building Self-confidence from Within

Self-confidence is an important factor of our success and happiness. This can help us take risks, pursue our goals, and overcome obstacles. However, many people struggle with self-doubt and low self-esteem which can set them back in different aspects of their life. In this chapter, we shall explore some effective strategies to build self-confidence from within.

Challenge negative self-dialogue

Negative self-discussion can be a significant obstacle to building self-confidence. This includes negative thoughts and beliefs about ourselves, such as, 'I am not good enough' or 'I always spoil things'. These thoughts can take up residence in our brains and prevent us from reaching our full potential.

One way of challenging negative self-dialogue is to recognise and question them. For example, if you think that you are not good enough, ask yourself, "Why do I believe this? What proof do I have to support this belief? Is there any other perspective that can be more accurate?"

Concentrate on strengths

Focusing on your strengths and achievements can also help in building self-confidence. Prepare a list of your strengths, skills and achievements and review them regularly. This can help to remind you of your abilities and achievements, which can increase your belief in your abilities.

Practice self-care

Self-care is necessary in order to build self-confidence. Self-care includes getting sufficient sleep, nutritious food, exercising regularly, and participating in activities that provide us with happiness and relaxation.

When we prioritise self-care, we prove to ourselves that we place importance on our well-being and respect it. This can help in increasing our self-confidence and self-respect.

Set attainable goals

Setting attainable goals and working towards them can also help in increasing self-confidence. When we establish goals and work towards them, we prove to ourselves that we are capable of achieving success.

It is important to set goals that are challenging but realistic. Setting challenging goals can become a reason for disappointment and frustration, whereas, setting effortless goals can feel unsatisfactory.

Practice visualisation

Visualisation is a powerful technique that involves imagining that we are successfully achieving our goals. This can help build self-confidence by creating an intellectual image of success and strengthening positive beliefs about our abilities.

In order to practice visualisation, close your eyes and imagine achieving your goals successfully. Imagine the places, sounds and sensations associated with your success. The more vivid and detailed your visualisation will be, the more effective it can be.

Take risks

Taking risks can also help in building self-confidence. When we step out of our comfort zone and try new things, we prove to ourselves that we are capable of facing challenges and achieving success.

However, it is important to take calculated risks instead of working impulsively. Before taking action, consider possible risks and gains and prepare a plan to deal with any obstacles.

Finally, building self-confidence from within is a process for which effort and practice are required. By challenging negative self-dialogue, focusing on our strengths, practising self-care, setting attainable goals, imagining success, and taking organised risks, we can build our self-confidence and achieve success in the various aspects of our life. Remember, building self-confidence is a lifelong journey, and when we work towards our goals, we must be patient and kind towards ourselves.

❑

15

Developing Consciousness in Daily Life

Consciousness is the practice of being aware of and present in the current moment without judgement or distraction. This can help you improve your intellectual health, reduce stress, and increase your overall health. Developing consciousness in your daily life is an important part of controlling your own mind. In this chapter, we shall explore some practical examples of how you can include consciousness in your routine.

Mindful breathing

Mindful breathing is one of the easiest and most effective ways of creating consciousness. Spare a few minutes every day to concentrate on your breathing and the sensation of the flow of air inside as well as outside your body. You can do this anywhere, anytime—when you are waiting for a bus, standing in a queue and even at your work desk. Here is an easy exercise that you can try.

Close your eyes and take a deep breath while feeling your chest and stomach expand. Hold your breath for a moment and then slowly release it, feeling the relaxation in your body. Repeat it for a few minutes. Focus only on your breathing and let any thought or distraction come and go, without judgement.

Food consciousness

Practising food consciousness can be a good opportunity to connect with your body. When you eat mindfully, you become aware of the sensations in your body as well as the taste and texture of the food. Some tips have been given here to help you eat mindfully.

Start taking a few deep breaths before eating food to help yourself relax and concentrate.

Focus on the colour, texture and smell of the food on your plate.

Take small bites and chew slowly, taste each morsel, and pay attention to how the taste and texture changes while chewing it.

Put down your fork or spoon while chewing food in order to slow down and help remain more present in the current moment.

Mindful walking

Walking is another activity that can be done with concentration. You can practice consciousness while walking by paying attention to your body and sensing your environment and atmosphere. Practice these simple steps.

Start by taking a few deep breaths and then walk slowly, while feeling each step.

Focus on the sensations of your feet as they touch the ground, your arm movements, and the flow of your breath.

Absorb the places and sounds around you while keeping in mind the colours, shapes and textures around you.

Try to remain present in the current moment without being trapped in thoughts or distractions.

Mindful communication

Mindful communication involves being fully present and alert while talking to others. This can help you develop strong relationships with the people around you and communicate more effectively with them. Some suggestions have been given here to practice mindful communication.

Give your full attention to the person with whom you are conversing. Listen actively and without any interruption.

Overcome any previous prejudice and obstinacy and try to be open as well as non-judgemental.

Along with your own body language and tone of voice, be conscious of the other person as well.

While speaking with kindness and compassion, spare some time to think about what had been said, before answering.

Mental work

Many of us spend plenty of time at work, which can be a stressful and distracting environment. By practising consciousness at work, you can gain help in focusing and being present as well as managing stress and anxiety. Some ways have been given here by which you can develop consciousness at your workplace.

Take a few moments at the beginning of each day to set your intentions and focus.

Take regular breaks for stretching, breathing or short walks outside.

Try to focus on one thing at a time, give it your full attention and avoid multitasking.

Be aware of your body and posture, and ensure that you are sitting or standing in a comfortable and relaxed position.

Use of mental techniques

In today's world, we are constantly surrounded by technology, which can often be a source of stress and anxiety. However, we can also use technology intelligently, as a tool to support our well-being and productivity. Some suggestions have been given here to use technology intelligently:

Set approximate boundaries for the use of technology such as switching off notifications for checking emails or social media or setting a specified time to check them.

Use technology in such a manner that it supports your welfare, such as using a meditation app or listening to soothing music.

Stay informed of how technology affects your mood or the level of your energy and adjust your use according to it.

Take a break from technology—go for a walk or spend time with nature.

Conscious self-reflection

Self-reflection is an important aspect of personal development and growth. Mindful self-reflection involves being honest and non-judgemental with yourself and open to learning and development. Some methods have been given here through which you can practice conscious self-reflection:

Spare some time every day to reflect upon your thoughts, emotions and work, without judging or criticising yourself.

Use journaling as an instrument for self-reflection. Write down your thoughts and emotions in a non-judgemental way.

Pay attention to the pattern in your thoughts and behaviour and consider how they are affecting your welfare and relationships.

Be open to feedback from others and use this as an opportunity for development and learning.

Conscious relaxation

Relaxation is an important part of self-care and can help you reduce stress and improve overall well-being. Mindful relaxation includes being fully present and alert during relaxation activities, such as bathing or listening to music. Some suggestions have been given here to practice mindful relaxation:

Create a relaxing atmosphere, such as dimming the lights or lighting candles.

Focus on the sensations in your body, such as the heat of the water or the vibration of the music.

Let go of any thought or distraction and just be present in this moment.

Practice self-compassion and let yourself relax completely, without feeling guilty or forced to do anything else.

Finally, developing consciousness in daily life can have an important effect on your welfare and overall happiness. By practising mindful breathing, eating, walking, communication, work, use of technology, self-reflection and relaxation, you can develop more understanding of presence and consciousness and become master of your own mind. Remember that consciousness is an exercise and takes time and patience to develop. Start small and with time, build the muscles of your consciousness slowly. With constant practice, you can change your daily life and experience more peace, happiness and satisfaction.

❑

16

Controlling Your Emotions

Emotions are an integral part of our human experience. They can bring happiness, enthusiasm and love in our lives but can also bring pain, anger and fear. Our emotions can be powerful and heavy, but we have the power to control and use them to our advantage. In this chapter, we shall explore ways of controlling our emotions and becoming masters of our minds.

Understanding your emotions

The first step in controlling your emotions is understanding them. Emotions are complex and can be affected by many factors, which include our prior experiences, present circumstances, and even our physical condition. It is essential to recognise and accept our emotions without judgement or resistance.

For example, if you are feeling worried, then accept this emotion and find the possible causes. Maybe there is a major upheaval in your work or you are worried about the health of a family member. By understanding the root of your feelings, you can start addressing them and find ways to manage them.

Managing your emotions

Once you understand your emotions, the next step is to learn how to manage them. There are different strategies to manage emotions and what works best, will differ from person to person. Here are a few examples:

Practice consciousness—Consciousness is the practice of being fully present and persevering in the moment, without judgement. By practising consciousness, you can be more aware of your emotions and learn to accept them without being overwhelmed.

Develop emotional intelligence—Emotional intelligence is the ability to recognise and understand your own feelings as well as those of others. By developing emotional intelligence, you can improve your communication skills and establish strong relationships with others.

Practice self-care—Taking care of yourself is an important part of managing your emotions. Ensure that you are taking adequate rest, consuming a healthy diet, and participating in those activities that make you happy.

Seek support—Sometimes, it can be difficult to manage your feelings. Do not hesitate to get help from friends, family or mental health professionals.

Using your feelings to your benefit

Once you have a better understanding of how to manage your emotions, you can start using them to your benefit. Emotions can be powerful motivators, and by learning to use them positively, you can achieve your goals and improve your life.

For example, if you feel angry about some injustice, use this anger to bring about a positive change. Join a social justice group or speak up against injustice creatively. If you feel excited about a new opportunity, use that excitement to lead yourself to success.

It is important to remember that feelings are not good or bad, they just happen. By learning to control your emotions, you can use their power and use them to build a more fulfilling life.

Finally, controlling your emotions is a continuous process that takes time, effort and self-consciousness. By understanding your emotions, learning to manage them, and using them to your benefit, you can become a master of your own mind and build a more fulfilling life.

Remember, it is fine to feel your emotions, even the inconvenient ones. By accepting them, you can control them and also use them to your benefit. Do not forget to seek help, if required. You do not have to travel this journey alone.

❑

17

Changing Inner Conflict

Inner conflict is an exercise of creating such problems or obstacles in our lives that prevent us from attaining our goals. It is a normal form of behaviour that can stop us from achieving success and happiness. Inner conflict can be manifested in many ways, such as delay, self-doubt and negative self-dialogue. Fortunately, inner conflict can be changed with a little effort and practice. In this chapter, we shall explore some of the most effective ways to change inner conflict.

Recognise the behaviour of your self-destruction

The first step in changing self-destruction is to identify those behaviours that are holding you back. Spare some time to reflect on your life and ask yourself which behaviours are preventing you from achieving your goals. Are you stalling on important tasks? Are you engaged in negative self-dialogue? Are you avoiding social situations? Once you identify your self-destructive behaviour, you can start taking steps to change it.

Change negative self-dialogue with positive self-dialogue

A negative self-dialogue is a usual form of inner conflict. It is the voice of our mind that tells us we are not good enough or will be unsuccessful. Negative self-discussion can weaken us and prevent us from taking action in the direction of our goals. The good news is that negative self-discussion can be changed with positive self-dialogue. Positive self-dialogue is the practice of using positive affirmations and quotes to counter negative self-discussion. For example, if you find yourself thinking 'I am not clever enough to do this', change it with 'I am capable of learning and growing'. By changing negative self-dialogue with positive self-dialogue, you can transform your intellect and start taking positive steps towards your goals.

Take action in the direction of your goals

Procrastination is another form of inner conflict. When we procrastinate, we postpone urgent work and responsibilities, which can lead to stress and anxiety. It is essential to take action in the direction of your goals in order to change procrastination. Divide your goals into small, manageable tasks and set a deadline for yourself. By taking action towards your goals, you can build momentum and create a sense of achievement, which can help to inspire you to move forward.

Take support from others

Inner conflict can be a lonely and isolated experience. It may feel as though only you are struggling with such behaviour. However, it is important to remember that you are not alone. Many people struggle with inner conflict. There is no shame in asking for help. Taking help from others can be a powerful way of changing inner conflict. Contact friends, family or doctors for support and guidance. Talking to a person who understands what you are doing can help you feel less alone and more inspired to overcome your self-destructive behaviour.

Practice self-care

Self-care is an important aspect of changing inner conflict. When we ignore our physical, emotional and intellectual health, we are more likely to engage in self-destructive behaviour. Take time for self-care activities such as exercise, meditation or spending time with nature. These activities can help in reducing stress and anxiety and improve our overall well-being. We can develop a positive basis for change and development by taking care of ourselves.

Examples of changing inner conflict

Let us consider some real-life experiences of people who have changed their self-destructive behaviour.

Example 1—Controlling procrastination

Sara was a writer who had always dreamt of publishing a novel. However, she constantly procrastinated and stopped writing. She would tell herself she was busy or needed to wait for the right inspiration. As a result, she did not make much progress on her novel. One day, Sara decided that enough was enough. She set a goal of writing 500 words every day for the next month. She divided her objective into small tasks such as outlining the plot of characters or writing character profiles. She set a specific time each day to work on her novel as well. By taking action towards her goal and dividing it into manageable tasks, Sara was able to overcome her procrastination and make significant progress on her novel.

Example 2—Changing negative self-dialogue with positive self-discussion

Vivek was a salesman who struggled with negative self-discussion. He would often say to himself that he was not good enough and would never be successful. This negative self-dialogue had a significant impact on his self-confidence and inspiration. Vivek started practising positive self-discussion in order to change his self-destructive behaviour. He would repeat positive affirmations to himself every day, such as 'I am capable of achieving my goals' or 'I am a successful salesman'. He began to transform his negative thoughts into more positive ones. For example, instead of thinking that 'I cannot make this sale' he would think 'I cannot make this sale but I can learn from this experience and do better next time'. He controlled his negativity by practising positive self-dialogue.

Example 3—Taking help from others

Kavita was a student who struggled with anxiety and self-doubt. She found it difficult to make friends and often felt isolated and lonely. Kavita decided to take support from others in order to change her self-destructive behaviour. She joined a student organisation that suited her interests and permitted her to meet like-minded people and make new friends. She began to consult a doctor as well, who helped her work through her anxiety and self-doubt. By taking support from others, Kavita was able to overcome her feelings of isolation and change her self-destructive behaviour.

Example 4—Practising self-care

Mika was a busy executive who would ignore his physical and emotional health. He worked long hours and skipped meals due to which he felt tired and stressed. Mika began to practice self-care in order to change his self-destructive behaviour. He took time for regular exercise and healthy food, due to which there was an improvement in his energy and mood. He also started practising consciousness meditation, which helped him manage his stress and anxiety. By giving priority to his self-care, Mika was able to change his self-destructive behaviour and improve his overall well-being.

Finally, changing self-destructive behaviour is not an easy task but is possible through some effort and practice. By recognising our self-destructive behaviour, practising positive self-dialogue, taking action towards our objectives, taking support from others, and practising self-care, we can transform our intellect as well as behaviour and achieve our goals. Remember, inner conflict is a normal experience, and there is no shame in asking for help. By taking steps to change our inner conflict, we can become masters of our own minds and build the lives we really want.

❑

18

Optimisation of Your Thought Pattern

Our thoughts have a powerful effect on our emotions, behaviour and overall well-being. Negative thought patterns can give rise to feelings of anxiety, depression and self-doubt, whereas, positive thought patterns can create feelings of happiness, self-confidence and inspiration. Optimising your thought patterns means keeping control over your thoughts and consciously choosing to focus on positive and empowered thoughts. In this chapter, we shall explore some strategies to optimise your thought patterns.

Practice gratitude

Gratitude is a powerful tool to optimise your thought pattern. When we focus on what we are grateful for, we remove our attention from negative thoughts and focus it on positive ones. We begin to appreciate the good things in life, which can help improve our overall mood and well-being. In order to practice gratitude, prepare a list of those things for which you are grateful every day. This can be a simple gesture, such as a good cup of coffee or a kind word from a friend. By focusing on the positive, you can begin to shift your thought pattern towards more empowered and positive people.

Challenge negative thoughts

Dealing with negative thoughts can be difficult and challenging. However, it is essential to recognise that our ideas are not always accurate or true. Challenging negative thoughts means questioning their validity and finding evidence to support or refute them. For example, if you think that you are not good enough, ask yourself, "What proof do I have to support this thought?" You can realise that there is no real evidence to support this idea and it is only a negative thought pattern. By challenging negative thoughts, you can start changing them with more positive and strong ones.

Imagine success

Visualisation is a powerful tool to optimise your thought pattern. When we imagine success, we prepare an intellectual image of achieving our goals that can help us improve our self-confidence and inspiration. In order to imagine success, close your eyes and imagine that you are achieving your goal. Imagine every detail, from pictures and sounds to feelings of accomplishment and satisfaction. By imagining success, you can begin to transform your thought pattern to make it positive and strong.

Practice affirmation

Affirmations are positive sayings that we repeat to ourselves in order to promote positive thought patterns. When we repeat affirmations, we start believing in them. This can help in improving our self-confidence and self-esteem. In order to practice affirmation, choose a positive saying that resonates with you, such as 'I am capable of achieving my goals' or 'I am worthy of love and respect'. Repeat this to yourself many times during the day. By practising affirmation, you can begin to transform your thought pattern to make it positive and strong.

Stay with positive people

Our environment can have a significant impact on our thought patterns. If we surround ourselves with negative people, then we can start adopting their negative ideas. On the other hand, if we surround ourselves with positive people, we can begin to adopt their positive ideas. In order to optimise your thought pattern, surround yourself with positive and helpful people who encourage and inspire you. Find such friends, family members or colleagues who have a positive outlook on life and share your goals and values.

Practice consciousness

Consciousness is the practice of being present in the moment and observing your thoughts without judgement. When we practice consciousness, we are more aware of our thought patterns and can begin to recognise negative thought patterns. Then, we can leave these negative thoughts and focus on the present moment. In order to practice consciousness, sit quietly for a few minutes every day and focus on your breathing. When thoughts arise, inspect them without judgement and then let go of them. By practising consciousness, you can begin to optimise your thought pattern and become a positive and strong intellectual.

Concentrate on solutions

It is easy to be trapped in negative thought patterns when one has to face challenges or problems. However, focusing on solutions can help in making your thought patterns positive and stronger. Instead of thinking about the problem, focus on finding solutions and taking action to solve the problem. Break the problem into small, more manageable steps and take action on every step. By focusing on solutions, you can begin to transform your thought pattern towards a more alert and positive intellect.

feel anxious or fearful. Instead of negating these feelings, try to accept them and understand that they are normal. This can help you take practical steps to manage your anxiety, such as practising relaxation techniques like meditation or taking deep breaths.

Reframe your intellect

Reframing your intellect is another way to embrace change and uncertainty. Instead of seeing change and uncertainty as negative experiences, try to see them as opportunities for growth and development. By reframing your intellect, you can focus on the positive aspects of change instead of the negative ones.

For example, if you face uncertainty in your career or personal life, try to see it as an opportunity to learn and grow. Maybe it is a chance to explore new career paths or hobbies you have always been interested in but did not have time for. By focusing on the positive aspects of the situation, you can develop a more optimistic outlook and enhance your flexibility for change.

Practice consciousness

Consciousness is an excellent tool to cope with change and uncertainty. By practising consciousness, you can develop more awareness about your thoughts and emotions, which can help you manage them more effectively. Consciousness can help you remain in the present moment, and you can focus on what you can control.

For example, if you are facing uncertainty in your personal life, try to practice consciousness meditation. This can help you remain in the present moment and avoid getting caught up in anxious thoughts about the future. By focusing on the present moment, you can feel more grounded and less overwhelmed by uncertainty.

Learn to adapt

The ability to adapt is an essential skill to embrace change and uncertainty. By learning to adapt, you can be prepared to manage unexpected situations in a more flexible and better way. Adaptability also involves being open to new ideas and experiences, which can help you grow and develop as a person.

For example, if you are facing an important change in your career, such as a new role or trade, try to be open-minded and adaptable. This may include learning new skills, networking with new people, or facing new challenges. You can enhance the possibility of your success and development by accepting change and being adaptable.

Seek support

Seeking support can help in dealing with change and uncertainty. It can be challenging to face these circumstances alone, and seeking support from friends, family or professionals can help you feel less alone and more supported.

For example, if you are facing an important change in your life, try to reach out to friends or family members for help. You can also consider getting professional help from a doctor or consultant who can provide you with guidance and help during this challenging time.

EXAMPLES OF CHANGE AND UNCERTAINTY

Changing career

Changing careers can be a difficult prospect for many people, especially if they are in one field or job for a long time. However, new opportunities for growth and development can open by embracing change and uncertainty.

For example, consider the matter of a software engineer who had been working in the tech industry for many years but felt dissatisfied and bored with his job. Despite his fear and uncertainty about changing his career, he decided to pursue his passion for music and took admission to a music production course. The resolve was challenging and he had to face a lot of uncertainty about the possibilities of his future career. However, by reframing his intellect and focusing on the positive aspects of the situation, such as receiving the opportunity to pursue his passion, he was able to adapt to change. Today, he is a successful music director and enjoys a fulfilling career, doing what he loves.

Relocating to a new city

Shifting to a new city can be a significant change. Adjusting to a new environment, meeting new people and establishing to a new routine can be challenging. However, by embracing change and uncertainty, you can change the experience into a positive one.

For example, consider the matter of a woman who had lived in the same small town for most of her life. She felt stuck in her routine and yearned for new experiences and opportunities. Despite her fear and uncertainty, she decided to relocate to a big city and embark on a new life. The resolve was challenging. She had to face a lot of uncertainty about her future in a new city. However, by practising consciousness, seeking support from friends and family, and learning to adapt to new circumstances, she could embrace change and change the experience into a positive one. Today, she is prospering in her new city, has made new friends, and experienced many new and exciting opportunities, which she would not have received while living in her old town.

The beginning of a new relationship

Beginning a new relationship can be both exciting as well as scary. It can be challenging to navigate the uncertainty of a new relationship, especially if you have been hurt in the past. However, you can open yourself to new experiences and possibilities by embracing change and uncertainty.

For example, consider the matter of such a person who was in a hostile relationship in the past and was afraid of being hurt again. Despite his fear and uncertainty, he decided to start dating again and met someone with whom he felt a strong connection. The resolve was challenging, and he had to face a lot of uncertainty about the future of the relationship. However, by accepting his feelings, practising meditation, and learning to adapt to the situation, he could embrace change and take a chance on love. Today, he is in a healthy and fulfilling relationship and is grateful that he took the risk and embraced the uncertainty of starting a new relationship.

Finally, embracing change and uncertainty is a necessary skill to become a master of your own mind. By accepting your feelings, reframing your intellect, practising consciousness, learning to adapt, and receiving support, you can accept change and convert uncertain situations into opportunities for growth and development.

Keep in mind that change and uncertainty are inevitable, but they should not be negative experiences. By adopting them, you can open yourself to new experiences and possibilities, which can help you become the best version of yourself.

❑

23

Developing a Clear Intellectual Vision

Have you ever felt that you are being swept away in life without any goal or a clear understanding of direction or objective? Without taking the time to consider where we want to go or what we want to achieve, it is easy to get stuck in the day-to-day tasks of life. However, a clear intellectual vision can be a powerful instrument to achieve success and fulfilment in life.

What is a clear intellectual vision?

A clear intellectual vision is a specific and well-defined image of what we want to achieve or become in our lives. This includes identifying our goals and aspirations as well as the necessary steps to achieve them. It also includes developing a positive intellect and visualisation technique in order to help us remain focused and inspired.

Why is a clear intellectual vision important?

A clear intellectual vision is important for many reasons. First, it helps us to remain focused on our goals and avoid distractions.

When we have a clear understanding of what we want to achieve, it becomes easy for us to prioritise giving our time and energy to work towards our objectives.

Second, a clear intellectual vision helps us to remain inspired despite obstacles and failures. When we face challenges or failures, we can remember our goals and remain committed to achieving them.

Finally, a clear intellectual vision helps us live a more purposeful and complete life. When we have an understanding of direction and objectives, we are more likely to feel a sense of accomplishment and satisfaction.

EXAMPLES OF BUILDING A CLEAR INTELLECTUAL VISION

Setting smart objectives

One way of building a clear intellectual vision is to set smart objectives. Smart goals are specific, measurable, attainable, relevant and timely. By setting goals that fulfil these criteria, we can build a clear intellectual vision of what we want and how we are planning to achieve it.

For example, if our objective is to reduce weight, then we can set the smart goal of losing ten pounds in three months, by exercising thrice a week, and eating nutritious food. This goal is specific, measurable, attainable, relevant and timely, by which it is easy to create a clear intellectual vision of our objective.

Visualisation technique

The second way of building a clear intellectual vision is to use visualisation techniques. Visualisation involves rehearsing our goals intellectually and imagining achieving them. This technique can help us to remain inspired and focused on our goals.

For example, if our goal is to run a marathon, we can imagine that we are running, crossing the finish line, and experiencing the feeling of accomplishment. By imagining achieving our goal, we can create a clear intellectual vision of what we want to attain and remain inspired to work for it.

Preparing a vision board

Preparing a vision board is another method of creating a clear intellectual vision. A vision board is a visual representation of our goals and aspirations. This can involve pictures, words and symbols that represent what we want to achieve.

For example, if we aim to travel to Europe, we can prepare a vision board with pictures of European places, maps of European countries, and travel quotes to inspire us. By preparing a visual representation of our goal, we can create a clear intellectual vision of what we want to achieve and remain inspired to work for it.

Finally, creating a clear intellectual vision is an essential tool to achieve success and fulfilment in our lives. By recognising our goals and aspirations, developing a positive intellect, and using visualisation techniques, we can create a clear intellectual vision of what we want to achieve and remain inspired to work towards our goals. There are many ways of creating a clear intellectual vision and becoming a master of your own mind, whether by setting smart goals, using visualisation techniques, or preparing a vision board.

❑

24

Setting Goals and Achieving Them

Goals are specific, measurable and attainable objectives that we set for ourselves. They represent our aspirations and desires and give us a sense of purpose and direction. Goals can be short-term or long-term and related to any aspect of our lives including our career, finance, health, relationships and personal development.

Why is it important to set goals?

Setting goals is important for many reasons. First, it helps us focus on what is important. When we have clear goals, we know what we want to achieve and can prioritise our time and energy accordingly.

Second, setting goals helps us to measure our progress and remain inspired. When we set measurable goals, we can track our progress and celebrate our accomplishments along the way. This helps us remain inspired and committed to achieving our goals.

Finally, setting goals helps us build a more complete and contented life. When we set and achieve meaningful goals, we experience a feeling of purpose and accomplishment, which can improve our overall well-being.

EXAMPLES OF SETTING AND ACHIEVING GOALS

Career goals

Setting career goals is one example of establishing goals and achieving them. If we want to advance in our careers, we can set specific goals which will help us achieve our objectives. For example, if we want a promotion, we can aim to acquire a new skill or certification, which will make us more valuable to our employer.

In order to achieve this goal, we can do a course or participate in a training programme, which will help us acquire the necessary skill. We can also work with an adviser or coach who can provide guidance and help us work in the direction of our goals.

Financial goals

Setting financial goals and achieving them is another example of how setting goals can help us build a more complete life. If we want to improve our financial situation, we can set specific objectives that will help us achieve our goals. For example, if we want to save money for the down payment of a house, we can aim to save a fixed amount every month.

In order to achieve this goal, we can prepare a budget that helps us manage our expenses and prioritise our savings. We can also explore ways to increase our income, such as doing a part-time job or starting a side business.

Personal development goal

Setting personal development goals and achieving them is another way of building a more complete life. If we want to improve ourselves and our personal relationships, we can set specific objectives that will help us achieve our goals. For example, if we want to be more vocal, we can set a goal of talking more in social situations.

In order to achieve this goal, we can practice speaking in small, less risky situations, such as with friends or family members. We can also work with a doctor or coach who can help us increase our self-confidence and develop effective communication skills.

Finally, setting goals and achieving them is a powerful tool to build a more complete and successful life. Whether we want to advance in our careers, improve our financial situation, or improve our personal relationships, setting goals can help us remain focused, measure our success, and remain inspired. By setting specific, measurable and attainable goals, and developing an effective strategy to achieve them, we can become masters of our own minds and create the life we want.

❑

25

Improve Decision-making Skills

We make countless decisions every day that affect our lives in a significant way. From deciding what to eat for breakfast to making important career or financial decisions, our ability to make good decisions is crucial to our success and happiness. However, it may be challenging to make decisions, especially when one has to face complex or high-stakes situations. In this chapter, we shall explore strategies to improve decision-making skills and make better choices.

Understand your decision-making style

The first step in improving decision-making skills is to understand our natural decision-making style. Some people are more analytical and logical, whereas others are more intuitive and emotional. By understanding our natural decision-making style, we can receive help in developing strategies to identify our strengths and weaknesses and make better decisions.

For example, if we make decisions based on emotions, we can benefit from adopting a more analytical approach to making decisions. This may include gathering more information, considering different options, and weighing the pros and cons of each option.

Develop decision-making process

Another strategy for improving decision-making skills is to develop one's decision-making process. This involves breaking the process of making decisions into specific stages and adhering to a structured approach to making decisions.

The following steps can be included in the process of making decisions:

The definition of the problem—Clearly define the problem or the decision to be made.

Research—Gather relevant information and data.

Options—Generate and evaluate different options.

Act—Choose the best option and take action.

Result—Evaluate the results of the decision and adjust as required.

By adhering to the process of making a structured decision, we can reduce the possibility of making impulsive or poorly thought-out decisions.

Use decision-making tools

Different decision-making tools and techniques can help us in making better decisions.

Examples

Decision matrix—A decision matrix involves preparing a table that lists different options and the criteria used to evaluate each option. This can help us weigh the options objectively and make more informed decisions.

List of pros and cons—This involves listing the pros and cons of every option to help us weigh the benefits and shortcomings of each of them.

Cost-benefit analysis—This involves evaluating the cost and benefits of each option in order to determine which option provides the greatest value.

Brainstorming—Brainstorming involves preparing a list initially of ideas or options without evaluating them. This can help us generate creative solutions and explore different possibilities.

Evaluate your decisions

After making a decision, it is important to evaluate it as well as its results. This can help us learn from our decisions and make better choices in the future.

A technique decision diary is to be used for evaluating decisions. This involves recording the decision, options considered, logic behind the decision, and results of the decision. By regularly reviewing our decision diary, we can identify patterns and improve our decision-making skills over time.

EXAMPLES OF IMPROVEMENT IN MAKING DECISIONS

Career decision

One example of improving decision-making skills is a career decision. While considering a job offer or career change, we can use decision-making processes to evaluate our options. This may involve researching different opportunities, evaluating the pros and cons of each option, and considering our long-term career goals.

We can also seek feedback from trusted advisers or peers and consider how each option aligns with our personal values and priorities.

Financial decision

Making the right financial decisions is another example of the significance of good decision-making skills. While making financial decisions, we can use tools such as cost-benefit analysis or a pros-cons list. We can also take advice from financial professionals or consult reputable sources of financial information.

By evaluating the possible results of each decision and considering our long-term financial goals, we can make the correct decision in line with our financial values and priorities.

Relationship decision

Making decisions in relationships can be challenging, especially when emotions are involved. However, we can use decision-making tools such as pros and cons lists or decision matrixes to evaluate different options as well as weigh the possible outcomes of each option.

We can also consider how each option aligns with our values and priorities. Take feedback from trusted friends or members of the family.

Health decision

Deciding on our health can be crucial for our overall well-being. When faced with health decisions, we can use decision-making tools such as cost-benefit analysis or decision matrix for evaluating different treatment options.

In order to ensure that we are making the correct decision in line with our health goals and values, we can take advice from healthcare professionals or consult reputable sources of health information.

Finally, improving decision-making skills is an important aspect of being a master of our own intellect. By understanding our natural style of making decisions, developing a process of making a structured decision, and using decision-making tools as well as techniques, we can make better decisions that would be in line with our values and priorities.

By evaluating our decisions and learning from our mistakes, we can improve our decision-making skills constantly and make more correct choices in all aspects of our lives.

❑

26

Enhancing Cognitive Abilities

Cognitive abilities are intellectual processes that enable us to gain, process, store and retrieve knowledge. These abilities include attention, memory, belief, logic, problem-solving and decision-making abilities. By enhancing these cognitive abilities, we can receive help to be more effective in our personal and professional lives. In this chapter, we shall explore some ways to enhance our cognitive abilities.

Being engaged in intellectual stimulation

Being engaged in intellectual stimulation can help in enhancing cognitive abilities. Intellectual stimulation includes activities that challenge the brain, such as reading, solving riddles, playing strategy games, and learning a new skill. These activities can help in improving memory, attention and problem-solving skills.

For example, attention and memory skills are required to read any book as well as understand and remember information. Problem-solving skills are required to solve riddles such as Sudoku or crossword. These enhance active memory. Playing strategy games such as chess can improve planning and decision-making skills.

Sufficient sleep

Getting enough sleep is essential for cognitive functions. Insufficient sleep can decrease attention, memory and problem-solving skills. Sleep plays a critical role in consolidating memories and eliminating toxic matter in the brain.

Getting seven to eight hours of sleep every night can help in improving cognitive abilities. Developing good sleep habits, such as setting a regular bedtime and avoiding electronic gadgets before sleeping can help in improving the quality of sleep.

Exercise

Exercise is good not only for physical health but also for cognitive functions. Exercising can increase the flow of blood in the brain which can enhance cognitive abilities. Exercise increases the production of brain-derived neurotrophic factor (BDNF) as well which helps in the development and survival of brain cells.

Participation in regular physical exercise such as walking, running or weightlifting can help enhance cognitive abilities. Even light exercise, such as yoga or Tai chi, can help improve attention, memory and problem-solving skills.

Nutritious food

Consuming nutritious food can also enhance cognitive abilities. The brain needs nutrients to function efficiently. A diet high in processed food products and sugar can reduce cognitive functions, whereas one high in fruits, vegetables and whole grains can increase cognitive functions.

Consuming a diet high in omega-3 fatty acids foods such as fish, nuts and seeds can help in improving cognitive functions. Omega-3 fatty acids are important for brain health and may improve memory, attention and problem-solving skills.

Meditation

Meditation is an exercise that involves focusing the mind on any specific object or activity, such as breathing or chanting. Meditation is said to improve attention, memory and problem-solving skills.

Meditation can help reduce stress and worry that can impair cognitive functions. It can also improve emotional regulation which can enhance decision-making skills.

Finally, it is important to enhance cognitive abilities in order to be masters of our own minds. Engaging in intellectual stimulation, getting sufficient sleep, exercising, consuming the right food, and meditation are some ways of enhancing cognitive functions.

By including these methods in our daily lives, we can improve our attention, memory, problem-solving and decision-making skills. We can be more effective in our personal as well as professional lives and achieve our goals more efficiently.

❑

27

Management of Time and Focus

Time is a precious commodity that we cannot waste. Managing our time and attention is more important than ever in today's fast-moving world. Time management is the process of effectively and efficiently methodising the way of allocating time and making plans to achieve our goals. Focus is the ability to concentrate on any task without being distracted by external or internal factors. In this chapter, we shall explore some ways of focusing time and attention.

Prioritising tasks

One of the most important aspects of time management is to prioritise tasks. Prioritisation involves identifying the most important tasks and completing them first. This helps in ensuring that we are progressing towards our goals and not wasting time on unimportant tasks.

In order to prioritise tasks, we can use tools such as the Eisenhower Matrix, which helps to separate urgent and important tasks from unnecessary and unimportant ones. Another method of prioritising work is using the Pomodoro technique, which involves breaking down tasks into intervals of twenty-five minutes and taking a five-minute break after each interval.

Eliminating distraction

Distraction can be a major time-waster and can make it difficult to focus on tasks. It is important to eliminate distractions as much as possible, in order to manage time and attention. This involves identifying possible distractions such as social media or email and exploring ways to reduce or eliminate them.

One way of eliminating distractions is to stop notifications on our electronic gadgets or set a specific time to check them. We can create a distraction-free environment even while working in a peaceful, organised space.

Using time-blocking

Time-blocking is a time management technique that involves scheduling specific blocks of time for specific tasks. This technique helps ensure that we concentrate on one task at a time and not get distracted by other tasks or activities.

In order to use time-blocking, we can prepare a schedule that includes blocks of time for different tasks or activities. For example, we can schedule two hours for work-related tasks in the morning, one hour for exercise, and another two hours for work-related tasks in the afternoon.

Delegating work

Delegating work is another method of managing time and focus. Delegation involves entrusting work to others who have the skills and resources to complete them. This helps in freeing our time and permits us to focus on tasks that require our unique skills and expertise.

In order to delegate work, we can identify those tasks that can be completed by others, and people and teams, who would have the necessary skills and resources, can be sought. We can also communicate our expectations clearly and provide the necessary support and feedback.

Taking breaks

Taking breaks is important for managing time and focus. This may appear contrary, but taking breaks can actually increase productivity and focus. This is so because taking breaks helps to prevent burnout and fatigue, which can impair cognitive functions and decrease productivity.

We can set specific times throughout the day to take breaks. We can also use techniques such as the Pomodoro technique, which involves taking a five-minute break after every twenty-five minutes of work.

Finally, managing time and attention is important for being a master of your own mind. By prioritising work, eliminating distractions, using time-blocking, delegating tasks, and taking breaks, we can manage our time and focus more effectively.

We can be more productive, achieve our goals more efficiently, and reduce stress and fatigue. We can control our time and attention with these techniques and be more effective and successful in our personal and professional lives.

❑

28

Fostering Healthy Relationships

Man is a social animal, and relationships play an important role in our lives. Healthy relationships can bring happiness, support and a sense of belonging in us, whereas unhealthy relationships bring stress and anxiety and can even harm us. In this chapter, we shall explore some ways of fostering healthy relationships.

Communication

Effective communication is the key to building and maintaining healthy relationships. Communication involves verbal and non-verbal signals, such as body language and tone. Good communication involves active listening, expressing yourself clearly and respectfully, and being open to feedback.

In order to improve communication, we can practice active listening by focusing on the speaker, summarising what he said as well as by asking clear questions. By using 'I said' instead of 'you said' and avoiding accusation and criticism, we can practice expressing ourselves clearly and respectfully.

Boundaries

Healthy relationships require boundaries that we set for ourselves as well as others. Boundaries help in establishing and maintaining respect, trust and mutual understanding. Healthy boundaries involve being clear about our needs and boundaries, expressing them clearly and respectfully, and being ready to negotiate and compromise.

In order to set healthy boundaries, we can identify our requirements and limits and communicate them clearly to others. We can be willing to listen to the needs as well as boundaries of others and if necessary, negotiate and compromise too.

Empathy

Empathy is the ability to understand and share the feelings of others. Empathy is important for building as well as maintaining healthy relationships because it helps establish trust, respect and compassion. Empathy involves active listening, acknowledging the feelings of others, and being willing to provide help as well as support.

In order to develop empathy, we can practice active listening by focusing on the speaker, acknowledging his feelings, and expressing empathy through words and actions. We can also practice placing ourselves in the position of others and imagining how they must feel in any specific situation.

Forgiveness

Forgiveness is the act of letting go of resentment and anger towards others who have hurt us. Forgiveness is important for maintaining healthy relationships because it helps establish trust, understanding and kindness. Forgiveness involves letting go of the past, accepting responsibility for your actions, and being willing to move forward.

In order to practice forgiveness, we can focus on the present moment and eliminate past complaints. We can also accept responsibility for our actions and if necessary, be willing to apologise and make amendments.

Respect

Respect is a basic aspect of healthy relationships. It involves treating others with dignity, kindness and consideration. Mutual respect is essential for healthy relationships, which involves acknowledging the ideas, feelings and needs of others.

In order to practice respect, we can treat others with compassion and consideration, listen actively and attentively, and avoid blame or criticism. We can be willing to compromise and negotiate and recognise the value and respect to others as well.

Finally, fostering healthy relationships reflects the positivity of our own intellect. By improving communication, establishing healthy boundaries, cultivating empathy, and practising forgiveness and showing respect, we can build or maintain healthy relationships that bring joy, support and fulfilment.

Healthy relationships can also help us deal with stress, overcome challenges, and achieve our goals. With these techniques, we can develop the necessary skills and intellect to nurture healthy relationships and become more effective and successful in our personal and professional lives.

❑

29

Enhancing Communication Skills

Communication is an important skill that is important for success in personal as well as professional life. It involves the give and take of information, thoughts and emotions between people. Effective communication skills permit us to build and maintain relationships, understand the perspective of others as well as achieve our goals. In this chapter, we shall explore some ways of enhancing communication skills.

Active listening

Active listening is an essential component of effective communication. It involves giving your full attention to the speaker and understanding the import of his message. Active listening includes focusing on the speaker, asking clear questions, and summarising what we have heard.

Example

Let us assume that we are in a meeting with our colleagues. In that situation, we can practice active listening by maintaining eye contact with the speaker, avoiding distractions, and summarising what we have heard. We can ask questions to clear any doubts we may have and express our understanding of the message of the speaker.

Unspoken communication

Body language, facial expressions and tone of voice are used to give messages in non-verbal communication. Non-verbal communication can increase or decrease the effectiveness of our communication. Positive non-verbal gestures can help in establishing relationships as well as expressing self-confidence and honesty.

For example, when we meet someone for the first time, we can use positive non-verbal gestures such as a firm handshake, smile and maintaining eye contact in order to express self-confidence and openness. We can also use suitable facial expressions and tone of voice to express empathy and understanding.

Written communication

Written communication involves the give and take of information through written words. Effective written communication skills are essential in today's digital age, where emails, memos and reports are ideal. Effective written communication involves clarity, conciseness and professionalism.

For example, let us assume we are writing an email to a colleague. In this situation, we can use clear and concise language, avoid grammatical errors, and use a professional tone. We can also use bullet points to highlight our chief information and make our message more readable.

Oral communication

Oral communication involves the use of spoken words in order to communicate a message. Effective oral communication involves clarity, self-confidence and a suitable tone. Effective communication skills are essential in situations such as public speaking, conversation and interviews.

For example, let us assume that we are giving a presentation to our team. In this situation, we can use clear and concise language, avoid word traps, and use a suitable tone to communicate our message. We can also use visual aids such as graphs and charts to make our message more compelling.

Empathy

Empathy involves acknowledging and sharing the feelings of others. Empathy is an essential component of effective communication because it helps establish harmony, trust and mutual understanding. Empathy involves active listening, acknowledging the feelings of others as well as expressing support and understanding.

For example, let us assume a colleague expresses disappointment about a challenging project. In that situation, we can practice empathy by listening actively, acknowledging his feelings, and expressing support as well as understanding. We can also give suggestions and help when appropriate.

Finally, it is essential to improve communication skills in order to be a master of your mind. Effective communication skills permit us to build and maintain healthy relationships, achieve our goals as well as understand the perspective of others. We can become effective communicators by practising active listening, using positive non-verbal gestures, improving our written and oral communication skills, and building empathy, as well as achieving success in our personal and professional lives.

❑

30

Building Resilience to Face Challenges

Life is full of challenges and we all have to face them at some point in our life. Whether it is a personal or professional jolt, we should learn how to navigate a difficult time and develop flexibility to bounce back strongly. Resilience is the ability to face and adapt to stress, adversity and change. In this chapter, we shall explore some ways to develop resilience in order to face challenges.

Developing an intellect for development

An intellect for development is a belief that our abilities and qualities can be developed and improved through hard work, dedication and determination. A development intellect permits us to see challenges as opportunities for development and learning, instead of insurmountable obstacles.

For example, if we are unsuccessful in any examination, we can see this as an opportunity to identify those areas where we need to improve and work hard. We can use the experience to develop a new strategy for studying and learning.

Practice self-care

Self-care involves taking care of our physical, emotional and intellectual health. The practice of self-care is necessary for developing resilience because it helps us manage stress, increase our energy level, and improve our overall health.

For example, we can practice self-care by doing regular exercise, getting sufficient sleep, eating nutritious food, and engaging in activities like meditation or reading.

Building a support network

Building a support network involves surrounding ourselves with people who care for us and are willing to give us support and encouragement during difficult times. A support network can provide us with emotional support, practical advice, and a sense of belonging.

For example, we can build a support network by joining a help group, reaching out to friends and family, or taking help from a professional consultant.

Setting realistic goals

Setting realistic goals involves setting attainable goals which are in line with our values and priorities. Setting unrealistic goals can give rise to a feeling of disappointment and failure which can hinder our ability to develop resilience.

For example, if we are recovering from an injury, we can set realistic goals for our rehabilitation such as increasing our movement slowly or recovering our strength in a specified period.

Learning from failure

Learning from failure involves reflecting on our mistakes as well as using them as opportunities for development and learning.

Failure is a natural part of life and it is important to see it as a learning experience instead of a jolt.

For example, if we are unsuccessful in an interview for a job, we can reflect on what went wrong and use the experience to improve our interview skills or identify those areas where we need to develop new skills.

Finally, the development of flexibility is essential for becoming masters of our own intellects. By developing an intellect of development, practising self-care, building a support network, setting realistic goals, and learning from failure, we can develop resilience to face challenges. Resilience permits us to adapt to change, avoid failure, and overcome obstacles by which we become stronger and more self-confident in our personal as well as professional lives.

❑

31

Self-discipline

Self-discipline is an essential skill to gain success in life. This involves the ability to control your thoughts, feelings and actions in order to achieve your goals and values. Constant effort and practice are required for self-discipline. It can be challenging to master it. However, by developing self-confidence, you can improve your productivity, increase your inspiration and achieve your goals more skillfully.

In this chapter, we shall explore the importance of self-discipline and provide you with some strategies as well as examples to help you master this important skill.

The importance of self-discipline

Self-discipline is important for several reasons:

Improves productivity

Self-discipline helps to prioritise your tasks and focus on the most important ones. It can improve your productivity by ensuring that you are effectively utilising your time and energy.

Increases motivation

Self-discipline helps you remain inspired by providing you with structure and routine. When you have a plan and abide by it, you are more likely to feel inspired to achieve your goals.

Builds flexibility

Self-discipline develops resilience by teaching you to stand firm through challenges and failures. When you are disciplined, you are better equipped to overcome obstacles and work towards your goals.

Improves self-control

Self-discipline helps you develop self-control by teaching you to counter those impulses and temptations that can derail your progress. This can help you make better decisions and avoid negative consequences.

STRATEGIES TO GAIN EXPERTISE IN SELF-DISCIPLINE

Set clear goals

Setting clear goals is an important first step in developing self-discipline. When you have a clear vision of what you want to achieve, it is easy to remain focused and inspired. Ensure that your goals are specific, measurable, attainable, relevant and timely. This will help you remain on track as well as measure your progress.

Prepare a plan

Once you set clear goals, it is essential to prepare a plan to achieve them. Divide your goals into small, manageable tasks and prepare a schedule to complete them. This will help you remain organised and focused and make it easy to track your progress.

Develop self-consciousness

Self-consciousness is a critical component of self-discipline. This involves being alert to your thoughts, feelings and actions and understanding how they affect your behaviour. By developing self-consciousness, you can identify those triggers that can give rise to delay, distraction or other behaviours, which can, in turn, weaken your self-discipline.

Practice self-control

Self-control is a critical component of self-discipline. This involves countering those impulses and temptations that can derail your progress. You can try techniques such as consciousness, deep breathing or visualisation to practice self-control. You can also create an environment that supports your self-control by eliminating distractions and temptations which can lead you astray.

Develop habits

Habits are a powerful instrument to develop self-discipline. When you develop such habits that support your goals, you can make progress without relying on willpower alone. Start small in order to develop habits and focus on continuity. Choose one habit to work on at one time and remain committed to practice it till it becomes automatic.

Examples of mastering self-discipline

In order to clarify the strategies that we have discussed, let us consider the examples of some people who have gained expertise in self-discipline and achieved their goals.

Ajit is an industrialist who has built a successful business. He credits his success to his self-discipline which he has developed by setting clear goals, preparing a plan and breaking down his tasks into small, manageable steps. Ajit also takes time every day to practice self-consciousness to reflect on his progress and identify the areas for improvement. He has developed habits that support his goals, such as waking early every morning and exercising before starting work. Ajit practices self-control as well, by avoiding those distractions and temptations that can hinder his productivity. By gaining expertise in self-discipline, Ajit has achieved his goals and built a thriving business.

Komal is a student who has developed excellent self-discipline. She sets clear goals for her academic performance and prepares a plan to achieve them. Komal practices self-consciousness too, by identifying her study habits and those areas where she can improve. She builds habits that support her goals, such as studying at the same time every day and using a planner to track her work. Komal practices self-control as well, by avoiding distractions and procrastination, which can hinder her study. By gaining expertise in self-discipline, Komal has achieved excellent academic results and is on her way to achieving her long-term career goals.

Saurabh is an athlete who has developed remarkable self-discipline. He sets clear goals for his training and competition and prepares a plan to achieve them. Saurabh practices self-consciousness too, by monitoring his progress and identifying those areas where he can improve. He builds habits that support his goals, such as training at the same time every day and focusing on his technique. Saurabh also practices self-control by avoiding temptations such as unhealthy food or excessive partying. By gaining expertise in self-discipline, Saurabh has become a top-performing athlete and has gained great success in his sport.

Finally, self-discipline is a necessary skill to achieve success in life. This requires continuous effort and practice but is a skill in which expertise can be gained. By setting clear goals, preparing a plan, developing self-consciousness, practising self-control, and building habits that support your goals, you can develop excellent self-discipline and achieve your goals. The examples we have explored show that by gaining expertise in self-discipline, you can achieve significant accomplishments in your profession, education, sports and other areas of life. So, start working on your self-discipline today and ensure your victory.

❑

32

Development of Inner Peace

Many people struggle to gain inner peace in today's fast-moving world. They are constantly attacked by stress, anxiety and negativity which can take a toll on their intellectual as well as emotional health. However, the development of inner peace is essential to achieve a sense of peace, balance and happiness in life. In this chapter, along with different strategies for cultivating inner peace, we shall explore examples of those people who have successfully applied them in their lives.

Practising consciousness

Practising consciousness is one of the most effective ways of developing inner peace. Consciousness is the practice of focusing on the present moment without judgement. It involves focusing on your breathing, sensations of the body and thoughts, without judging them. By practising consciousness, you can learn to be more aware of your thoughts and feelings as well as develop a sense of inner peace.

Jaya is one such person who has successfully developed inner peace through consciousness. Jaya practices consciousness through daily meditation and yoga. She also consciously disconnects from technology and spends time with nature. Through these modes, Jaya has developed a great feeling of self-consciousness and inner peace.

Practice gratitude

Practising gratitude is another effective strategy for the development of inner peace. This involves focusing on the positive aspects of your life and being grateful for them. By practising gratitude, you can remove your focus from negative thoughts and emotions and develop a great sense of inner peace and satisfaction.

Vijayan is one such person who has successfully developed inner peace through gratitude. Vijayan practices gratitude by writing three things every day for which he is grateful. He also takes time to reflect on the positive aspects of his life, such as his health, relationships and accomplishments. Through these practices, Vijayan has developed a more positive approach to life and a great sense of inner peace.

Self-care

Another effective way of developing inner peace is engaging in self-care. This involves taking care of your physical, intellectual and emotional welfare. It can include activities like exercise, eating nutritious food, getting sufficient sleep, and engaging in hobbies or activities which give you happiness.

Komolika is one such person who has successfully developed inner peace through self-care. Komolika prioritises self-care through regular exercise, eating nutritious food, and spending time with loved ones. She also takes time to reflect on her accomplishments and practice self-compassion. Through these practices, Komolika has developed a great feeling of inner peace and self-confidence.

Let go of negative thoughts and emotions

Letting go of negative thoughts and emotions is another effective strategy in order to develop inner peace. Negative thoughts and emotions can be sources of stress and anxiety and can prevent you from experiencing a sense of inner peace and satisfaction.

Deepak is one such person who has successfully developed inner peace by letting go of negative thoughts and feelings. Deepak practices accepting his negative thoughts and emotions and letting go of them through meditation and visualisation. He also practices self-compassion by accepting himself and embracing his strengths and weaknesses. Through these practices, Deepak has developed a great sense of inner peace and balance.

Finally, developing inner peace is essential for achieving a sense of peace, balance and happiness in life. This requires continuous effort as well as practice but the rewards are worth it. By practising consciousness, gratitude and self-care as well as letting go of negative thoughts and emotions, you can develop a great sense of inner peace and well-being. You can also be a source of inspiration for others by sharing your story with them and encouraging them to develop inner peace in their lives. Keep in mind that inner peace is not only a state of mind; rather, it is a way of living life. Embrace it and enjoy great peace.

❑

33

Finding Purpose and Meaning

Finding purpose and meaning in life is essential for gaining a sense of fulfilment and happiness. However, many people struggle to find what creates a feeling of dissatisfaction and disappointment. In this chapter, we shall explore different strategies to find purpose and meaning and also provide examples of such people, who have successfully found them in life.

Identify your values

The first step in finding purpose and meaning in life is to identify your values. Your values are those principles and beliefs which are most important to you. They provide a sense of direction and guide your decisions and actions.

Kamal Kumar is one such person who has found purpose and meaning by successfully identifying his values. Kamal's values include authenticity, courage and kinship. He has dedicated his life to teaching others about vulnerability and authenticity and how they can take their lives towards more fulfilment. Through his work, Kamal has found a sense of purpose and meaning by helping others live a more authentic and full life.

Pursue your passion

Pursuing your passion is another effective strategy for finding purpose and meaning in your life. Your passions are activities and interests that provide you happiness and satisfaction. By pursuing your passion, you can utilise your creativity and talent and achieve a sense of purpose and meaning in your life.

Premchand is one such person who has successfully found purpose and meaning by pursuing his passion. Premchand's passion for writing inspired him to write many timeless stories such as 'Kafan' and *Godan* which provided happiness and inspiration to millions of people throughout the world. Through his work, Premchand found purpose and meaning in inspiring others and writing stories that inspire them.

Serve others

Serving others is another effective way to find purpose and meaning in life. When you serve others, you can exert a positive influence in the world and contribute to something bigger than yourself. Serving others can also help you develop a feeling of sympathy and compassion.

Baba Ramdev is one such person who has successfully found purpose and meaning by serving others. Through his charitable work, Ramdev has dedicated his life to improvement in global health and poverty eradication. Through his foundation, he has helped provide access to life-saving medicines to millions of people in the world. Through his work, Ramdev has found a sense of purpose and meaning in making a positive impact in the world.

Embrace challenges and adverse circumstances

Embracing challenges and adversity is another effective way to find purpose and meaning in life. When you face challenges and adverse situations, you are forced to develop new skills and abilities. This can create a greater understanding of purpose and meaning in your life because you learn to overcome obstacles and achieve your goals.

Mary Kom is a person who has successfully found purpose and meaning by embracing challenges and adverse circumstances. Mary had to face many challenges and obstacles including poverty, ill-treatment and discrimination in her life. However, she persevered and became one of the most successful boxers in history. Through her work, Mary has found a sense of purpose and meaning in empowering others to rise from challenges as well as achieve their dreams.

Finally, it is essential to find purpose and meaning in life to gain a sense of fulfilment and happiness. This requires continuous effort and practice, but the rewards are worth it. By identifying your values, pursuing your passion, serving others, and embracing challenges as well as adverse circumstances, you can gain more understanding of the purpose and meaning in your life. You can also be a source of inspiration for others by sharing your story with them and encouraging them to find purpose and meaning in their life. Keep in mind that you have a purpose and the power to make your life meaningful. Implement it and achieve the desired success.

❑

34

Developing Self-Reflection

Self-reflection is the practice of looking inwards and examining your thoughts, feelings and behaviour. This is an essential tool for personal growth and development by which people can attain self-consciousness and bring about a positive change in their lives. In this chapter, we shall discuss the benefits of developing self-reflection and provide practical examples of including self-reflection in our routine.

Enhancement in self-consciousness

An enhancement in self-consciousness is one of the most important benefits of self-reflection. By consciously considering your thoughts and feelings, you can gain a deep understanding of your values, strengths and weaknesses. This enhanced self-consciousness can help you make better decisions and improve your relationship with others.

For example, if you observe that you are often angered when someone disagrees with you, then self-reflection can help you develop strategies to identify the basic reason for your anger and manage it in a better manner in the future.

Better problem-solving skills

Self-reflection can also help in improving problem-solving skills. By reflecting on past experiences and examining your thought processes, you can identify those patterns of behaviour that can hinder your ability to solve problems effectively.

For example, if you observe that you reach the conclusion straightaway, without considering all the facts, then self-reflection can help you be more conscious of your thought processes and develop a more systematic approach to problem-solving.

Making better decisions

Self-reflection can also give rise to the skill of making better decisions. By reflecting on your values, priorities and goals, you can make decisions that align with your values and contribute to your long-term success and happiness.

For example, if you are considering a job offer that pays well but is not in line with your values, then self-reflection can help you make a decision of what is best for you, even if it means turning down the job offer.

Enhancement of emotional intelligence

Self-reflection can also enhance emotional intelligence. Emotional intelligence is the ability to recognise and manage your own feelings as well as those of others. By reflecting on your own feelings, you can develop more sympathy and understanding for the feelings of others.

For example, if you notice that you often feel anxious in social situations, then self-reflection can help you develop strategies to manage your anxiety and be more attuned to the feelings of others in social situations.

Personal growth

Self-reflection can also lead to more personal growth. By reflecting on your past experiences and examining your present behaviour, you can identify areas of improvement and develop a strategy to bring about a positive change in your life.

For example, if you notice that you often procrastinate in important tasks, then self-reflection can help you develop strategies to identify the basic reason for your laxity and eliminate it.

Better relationships

Self-reflection improves all relationships. By reflecting on your thoughts, feelings and behaviour, you can be more aware of how you talk to others and develop strategies to improve your communication and relationship skills.

For example, if you observe that you often interrupt others when you are speaking, then self-reflection can help you develop strategies to be more aware of this behaviour and listen more carefully as well as communicate more effectively.

Finally, self-reflection is an essential tool for personal development. By including self-reflection in your daily routine, you can achieve self-consciousness, improve problem-solving skills, make better decisions, enhance emotional intelligence, experience more personal development, and improve your relationship with others. In order to develop self-reflection, try to set aside a few minutes every day to reflect on your thoughts, feelings and behaviour. With practice, self-reflection can become a natural and profitable part of your routine.

❑

35

Ability to Focus Attention

The ability to concentrate is an important skill for success in all aspects of life, from educational and professional activities to personal goals and relationships. However, in today's world of constant distractions, it is becoming increasingly challenging to gain mastery in the art of concentration. In this chapter, we shall discuss the benefits of gaining expertise in the art of concentration and provide practical examples for improving focus.

Better productivity

One of the most important benefits of gaining mastery in the art of focus is better productivity. When you can focus on any job without being distracted, you can complete it more skillfully and effectively. This enhanced productivity can lead to better results in both personal and professional activities.

For example, if you are working on a project for work and can focus on it without being distracted by email, social media or other interruptions, then you are more likely to complete the project on time and on a high level.

Enhanced creativity

Creativity can also be enhanced by mastering the art of focus. When you are fully engaged in any task, you can enter a state of flow where ideas and inspiration come naturally. This state of flow can lead to enhancement in creativity and novelty.

For example, if you are a writer, mastering the art of focus can help you enter the state of flow, where you can write more freely and creatively, without being distracted by external influences.

Better memory

Another benefit of mastering the art of focus is memory improvement. When you can focus on any task without being distracted, you are more likely to remember the details of the work and retain the information.

For example, if you are studying for any examination, then mastering the art of focus can help you retain the information that you are reading and remember it easily during the examination.

Less stress

Stress can also be reduced by mastering the art of focus. When you are distracted by external influences, you can be overwhelmed and stressed. However, when you focus on any work, you can enter a state of flow, which is calm and focused.

For example, if you are feeling stressed at work, mastering the art of focus can help you enter the state of flow, where you can concentrate on your work and feel less overwhelmed.

Better relationships

Gaining expertise in the art of focus can lead to improvement in relationships as well. When you can concentrate on a conversation or activity without being distracted, you can be fully present in that moment and connect more deeply with others.

For example, if you are talking to a friend, then mastering the art of focus can help you listen more carefully and answer more thoughtfully, which forms a deep bond with your friend.

PRACTICAL EXAMPLES OF IMPROVEMENT IN FOCUS

Set goals and prioritise work

Setting goals and prioritising work can help you focus on the most important tasks and avoid distractions. Start by setting attainable goals and dividing them into small tasks. Then, prioritise tasks based on their importance and complete them at one go.

Eliminate distractions

Eliminating distractions can help you focus on your work. Shut off the notifications on your phone, close unnecessary tabs on your computer, and work in a peaceful environment.

Practice consciousness

By practising consciousness, you can be more aware of your thoughts and feelings and improve your ability to focus. Try to meditate for a few minutes every day or practice deep breathing exercises.

Take breaks

Taking breaks can help you recharge and refocus. In order to refresh your mind, take a short walk, do some stretching exercises, or participate in relaxing activities.

Use time management techniques

By using time management techniques, you can make the most of your time and avoid procrastination. Try to use the Pomodoro technique, in which you work for twenty-five minutes and then take a five-minute break, or the Eisenhower Matrix, which helps you prioritise tasks based on their urgency and importance.

Practice single-tasking

Practising single-tasking can help you focus on one task at one time and avoid multitasking, which can break concentration and decrease productivity. Before going on to the next task, try to focus on one task till it is completed.

Sufficient sleep

Getting sufficient sleep is important for improvement in focus and concentration. In order to help feel more alert and focused during the day, set a goal of sleeping for seven to eight hours every night.

Finally, mastering the art of focus is an essential skill for success in all aspects of life. By improving your focus, you can increase your productivity and creativity, improve memory, reduce stress, and improve relationships. By practising techniques such as setting goals, eliminating distractions, practising consciousness, taking breaks, using time management techniques, practising single-tasking, and getting sufficient sleep, you can get help in focusing and achieving your goals. Keep in mind, that gaining expertise in the art of focus is a continuous process, and it takes time and practice to develop this skill.

❑

36

Manifesting Creativity

Creativity is an essential skill that enables people to come up with unique and fresh ideas that can help in solving problems, improving products and services, and making life more enjoyable. However, many people believe that only some people have creativity and it is not something that can be learnt. This belief is not true because creativity is a skill that can be developed and refined with practice.

In this chapter, we shall discuss some effective ways to manifest your creative ability and be more innovative in your personal as well as professional life.

Brainstorming

Brainstorming is a popular technique that helps people generate new ideas by encouraging them to think creatively and express their ideas freely. This involves gathering a group of people and asking them to come up with more and more ideas on the given topic, without criticism and judgement. Brainstorming sessions can be done in person or virtually and can help you manifest your creativity by processing your mind and opening it to new ideas.

Example—A marketing team is brainstorming ideas for a new advertisement campaign for a product. Each member of the team is encouraged to share ideas freely, without criticism and the team leader writes all the ideas on a whiteboard. The team then evaluates each idea and chooses the most novel and effective one.

Mind mapping

Mind mapping is a technique that helps people to visually organise their ideas. This involves preparing a map or diagram that connects different ideas, concepts and information in a structured way. Mind mapping can help in manifesting your creative ability by enabling you to explore different ideas and connections, which you would not have otherwise considered.

Example—A writer uses mind mapping to organise his ideas and perspective for a new book. He starts with the central idea and then forms branches, which represent different characters, subjects and plot points. A mind map enables a writer to see how the different elements of the story join together and inspire new and creative ideas.

Stepping out of comfort zone

Stepping out of your comfort zone is a powerful way to manifest creativity. When you take risks and try new things, you open yourself to new experiences, perspectives and ideas, which can inspire creativity. Trying new things can also help you eliminate fear, self-doubt and other intellectual obstacles that can affect creativity.

Example—A graphic designer is stepping out of his comfort zone by learning new design software. By learning this new software, the designer opens himself to new design possibilities, which he would not have previously considered.

Collaborating with others

Collaborating with others can help manifest your creative ability by bringing different perspectives, skills and ideas to the table. Collaborating with others can help you learn from their experiences, gain new insight and explore new ways of thinking.

Example—A team of engineers is collaborating to design a new product. Each engineer brings a unique perspective and set of skills for the project, by which they are able to develop new ideas, which they could not have come up with by themselves.

Taking breaks

Taking breaks is an easy but effective way to manifest your creativity. Taking breaks can help you recharge your mind and reduce stress, which can help promote creativity. During the break, you can participate in those activities which help you relax, such as taking a walk, listening to music, or practising meditation.

Example—A painter takes a break from painting to walk in nature. The walk helps the painter to relax and clear his mind, by which he can return to his painting with a fresh perspective.

Conclusion

Manifesting your creative ability is an essential skill that can help you solve problems, improve products and services, and make life more enjoyable. By using techniques such as brainstorming, mind mapping, stepping out of your comfort zone, collaborating with others, and taking breaks, you can tap into your creativity and develop new ideas. Keep in mind that creativity is not something that only a few people possess. This is a skill that can be developed and mastered with practice. Therefore, in order to manifest your creativity, do not be scared of trying new things, taking risks, and collaborating with others.

❑

37

Ease in Adversity

Adversity is an inevitable part of life. It can appear in different forms, such as challenges, failures and losses. No one is safe from adversity, and every person faces it at some point in their life. However, what separates successful people is their ability to overcome adverse circumstances and develop resilience. Resilience is the intellectual and emotional ability to deal with difficult situations and recover from them and an important skill to master your own mind.

Flexibility is not something with which you are born; rather, it is a skill that can be developed and strengthened with time. Self-consciousness, consciousness and an active intellect are necessary for building resilience. This involves developing a healthy coping strategy, managing emotions effectively, maintaining a positive outlook, and developing an intellect of development. Let us examine some examples of how people can build resilience in order to face adverse circumstances.

Development of healthy coping strategies

Developing a healthy coping strategy to deal with adverse circumstances is one of the main aspects of building resilience.

Coping strategies are the ways in which we manage and respond to stress in our lives. Healthy coping strategies are those that are adaptive and creative and promote welfare. They help us navigate difficult circumstances effectively, without succumbing to negative feelings or behaviour.

For example, when we have to face a challenging situation such as the loss of a job, a resilient person can use healthy coping strategies, such as seeking support from friends and family, focusing on his strengths and skills, and exploring new opportunities. He can also engage in self-care activities such as exercise, meditation and hobbies, in order to manage stress and maintain emotional well-being. As opposed to this, a person who lacks resilience can rely on unhealthy coping strategies, such as excessive drinking, evasion or self-blame, which can further increase the problem and hinder his ability to return.

Managing feelings effectively

Emotional intelligence is another factor in building resilience. Emotions are a natural part of being human and it is important to accept and manage them effectively while facing adverse circumstances. Emotionally resilient people are aware of their feelings, can control them and instead of being overwhelmed, can use them as a source of inspiration and power.

For example, while facing a shock or failure, a resilient person can permit himself to feel disappointment or frustration but will not focus on it for a very long time. He can practice self-compassion and accept that it is fine to feel like this, but he also reminds himself of his previous successes and strengths. He can also change the situation into an opportunity to learn and focus on finding the solution to the problem, instead of the problem itself. As opposed to this, a person who struggles with emotional resilience can be overwhelmed by negative feelings such as self-doubt or anger. He may have to struggle to move forward, which may lead to crises and poor decisions in the long run.

Maintaining a positive outlook

A positive outlook is an integral factor of resilience. This involves maintaining a positive intellect even in adverse circumstances and searching for a ray of hope in difficult situations. A positive outlook does not mean negating the reality of a situation or avoiding negative feelings; rather, it is adopting an approach focused on possibilities, opportunities and solutions.

For example, when a resilient person faces a challenging situation, such as a breakup or a health problem, he can focus on the lessons learnt, achieve personal development, or get support from others. He can explore ways of changing the situation in a positive light and maintaining hope and optimism. He can also practice gratitude and count his blessings, which changes his perspective to appreciate the positivity in his life in adverse circumstances. On the other hand, a person who lacks a positive outlook can focus on negativities, complain constantly or blame others, and have a pessimistic outlook about the future. This negative intellect can hinder his ability to face adverse circumstances and find solutions, which in turn, reduces positivity and resilience.

Building a development intellect

A development intellect is a belief that challenges and failures are opportunities of development and learning instead of fixed boundaries. This involves adopting an intellect that is open to learning, adaptive and willing to adopt change. Developing an intellect of development is important for building resilience because it permits people to see challenges as opportunities for development instead of insurmountable obstacles.

For example, while facing failure or a shock, a person with an intellect of resilience and development can see it as an opportunity to learn from his mistakes, gain new skills, or change his approach. He can see it as a step towards success, instead of a roadblock. He can also be willing to take risks, try new things and adopt his strategies, based on feedback and experiences. As opposed to this, a person with a decided intellect can view failure as a reflection of his abilities or capability, feel defeated, and be resistant to learning from change or experience.

Illustration of past resilience

Another powerful way to build resilience in crisis is to draw on (reflect on) past experiences of resilience. Considering past challenges that you have successfully overcome can serve as a reminder of your inner strength and resilience. It can help you gain perspective and self-confidence in your ability to deal with current adversity.

For example, think about the time when you faced a difficult situation, such as a breakup, loss of job, or health scare, and successfully navigated through it. Which coping strategies did you use? How did you manage your feelings? Did you maintain a positive outlook or adopt a development intellect? Reflecting on your past resilience can remind you of those skills and strategies that work for you and assure you that you can overcome the current adversity as well.

Seeking support from others

Building resilience does not mean facing adverse circumstances alone. Seeking support from others is an important aspect of resilience. This involves reaching out to friends, family or professionals for guidance, encouragement and sympathy. Social support can provide a buffer against the negative effects of adverse circumstances and can help people face them more effectively.

For example, while facing a challenging situation such as loss or a big life change, a resilient person can actively gain support from trusted people. He can talk about his feelings and anxieties, take advice, or someone can be there to listen to him. He can join help groups or gain professional help, such as treatment or consultation, as well as other tools and strategies for coping. As opposed to this, a person who isolates himself or refuses to take support can struggle to face adversity on his own and can feel overwhelmed or helpless.

Practice self-care

Self-care is an integral element of building resilience. It is important to take care of your physical, intellectual and emotional welfare in times of trouble. The practice of self-care can help you manage stress, maintain a positive outlook, and build the necessary inner resources to effectively deal with adverse circumstances.

For example, during difficult times, a person with flexibility can give priority to self-care activities, such as getting sufficient sleep, eating nutritious food, exercising regularly, and practising relaxation techniques like meditation or deep breathing. He can also participate in those activities that provide him happiness and satisfaction, such as hobbies, spending time with loved ones, or pursuing a creative outlet. Self-care practices can fill you with energy, enhance your mood, and improve your overall well-being, which in turn, can help you build resilience and navigate through adversity.

Finally, building resilience in adverse circumstances is an important skill that can empower you to be a master of your own mind. This is a continuous process that requires deliberate effort and practice. By developing a positive intellect and coping skills, accepting change, gaining support from others, and practising self-care, you can strengthen your resilience and navigate life's challenges effectively.

Keep in mind that resilience is not about avoiding adversity or negating it; rather, it is about facing it and overcoming it. It is about developing intellectual and emotional resilience that is adaptive to change, the ability to learn from failures, and the desire to seek support, if need be. Resilience is a powerful tool that can empower you to overcome adverse circumstances, face challenges, and live a complete and flexible life.

Therefore, as you continue your journey to control your mind, remember to prioritise building resilience in adverse circumstances. Embrace challenges as opportunities for development, adopt a positive intellect, draw on past experiences of resilience, seek support from others, and practice self-care. With resilience as your foundation, you can navigate through the ups and downs of your life with kindness and strength and ultimately, become masters of your own minds.

❑

38

Creating Joy and Happiness

Happiness is an essential factor in a full life. It not only adds richness and meaning to our experiences but also contributes to our overall welfare and intellectual health. Happiness and creating happiness is a lifelong journey that requires deliberate effort and change in intellect. In this chapter, we shall explore happiness and its importance, the factors that affect our happiness, and practical strategies, to create more joy and happiness in our lives.

Importance of joy and happiness

Happiness and joy are often used interchangeably, but they are different emotions. Happiness is a deep-seated emotion that arises from within, often as a result of positive experiences or relationships with others. This is a feeling of inner joy, satisfaction and gratitude that is beyond external circumstances. On the other hand, joy is a broad concept encompassing a general sense of well-being and satisfaction with life. This can arise from different sources such as accomplishments, relationships and personal values.

Both joy and happiness have an important effect on our intellectual, emotional and physical health. Research has shown that there can be many benefits of experiencing joy and happiness, which include:

Better intellectual health—Joy and happiness can reduce symptoms of anxiety, conflict and stress. They enhance positive emotions which are associated with better intellectual health results and resilience.

Improved physical health—Joy and happiness are related to better physical health results which include low blood pressure, better immune functions, and reduced risk of chronic ailments like heart disease.

Strong relationships—Joy and happiness contribute to positive social relationships and deep relationships with others. They can improve our relationships and enhance our sense of community and belonging.

Increase in productivity and creativity—Joy and happiness can increase inspiration, creativity and productivity, by which, we can be more successful in different areas of life including work, hobbies and personal goals.

Life satisfaction—Joy and happiness are fundamental to overall life satisfaction. When we experience joy and happiness, we view our lives more positively and feel an enhanced sense of well-being and fulfilment.

Factors that influence happiness

Happiness is a complex and multidimensional emotion that is influenced by different factors. Whereas genetics and external circumstances play a role in the level of our happiness, research has shown that our thoughts, behaviour and intellect have a significant impact on our happiness as well. Some factors that affect our happiness have been given here:

Intellect—Our intellect or perspective towards life plays an important role in our happiness. Gratitude, optimism and a positive intelligence characterised by resilience can enhance joy and happiness.

Relationships—Our relationships with others including family, friends and social relationships are an integral part of our happiness. Positive and supportive relationships can contribute to our overall welfare and happiness.

Self-care—Taking care of our physical, intellectual and emotional health is important for our happiness. Regular exercise, sufficient sleep, healthy nutrition, and self-compassion are essential components of self-care, which can contribute to our happiness.

Meaning and purpose—Having a sense of purpose and meaning in life can have a profound impact on our happiness. Participating in activities that align with our values, beliefs and interests can give us a feeling of satisfaction and joy.

Practical strategies for creating joy and happiness

Creating joy and happiness requires deliberate effort and practice. Some practical strategies have been given here that can help you create more joy and happiness in your life:

Foster positive relationships—Surrounding yourself with positive and supportive relationships can profoundly impact your happiness. Spend time with loved ones, participate in meaningful conversations, and express gratitude and praise towards others. Fostering healthy relationships and maintaining them can contribute to your overall welfare and bring happiness to your life.

Practice gratitude—Gratitude is a powerful tool to create joy and happiness. Practice acceptance of positivity in your life and expressing gratitude through its appreciation, however small it may appear to be. Gratitude can focus your attention on what you have and enhance your overall sense of well-being and happiness.

Remain engaged in activities that bring happiness—Identify those activities that give you happiness and take out time for them in your life. This can be something as simple as spending time with nature, joining a hobby, listening to music, or spending quality time with loved ones. Make a conscious effort to give priority to and engage in those activities that give you happiness and make them a regular part of your routine.

Practice self-compassion—Treat yourself with the same kindness, understanding and compassion that you would offer a dear friend. Be gentle with yourself, accept your flaws and practice self-acceptance. Avoid self-criticism and negative self-discussion and instead, focus on self-care and self-compassion. When you are kind towards yourself, you are more likely to experience joy and happiness.

Focus on the present moment—Being present in the current moment and fully experiencing the present is important for happiness and creating happiness. Avoid remaining in the past or worrying about the future because it can hinder your ability to experience joy in the present moment. Practice consciousness and focus on what you are doing, feeling and experiencing in the current moment.

Practice kindness and compassion—Practising kindness and compassion towards others can also contribute to your joy and happiness. Remain engaged in acts of kindness, provide others with help and support, and practice sympathy and compassion. Kindness and compassion not only benefit others but also create a wave of positivity in your life which increases joy and happiness.

Set meaningful goals and pursue them—Setting meaningful goals and pursuing them can give you a sense of purpose and fulfilment which gives you much joy and happiness. Reflect on your values, interests and passions and set realistic and attainable goals that align with them. Pursue your goals with inspiration and determination and celebrate your progress along the way. The process of pursuing meaningful goals can bring joy and happiness in your life.

Take care of your physical health—Our physical health is closely associated with our intellectual and emotional welfare. Taking care of your physical health such as exercising regularly, eating healthy food, and getting sufficient sleep can contribute to your overall well-being and sense of happiness. Take care of your body by participating in regular physical activities that you enjoy, eating nutritious food products that give fuel to your body, and giving priority to quality sleep. When you feel good physically, you are more likely to experience joy and happiness in your daily life.

Practice forgiveness—Anger and holding grudges can make you stressed as well as hinder you from real happiness and experiencing happiness. Practice forgiveness towards others as well as yourself. Let go of past sorrows, accept that shortcomings and mistakes are a part of being human, and grant forgiveness as well as compassion to yourself and others. Forgiveness can liberate you from emotional burdens and make place for joy and happiness to thrive.

Develop positive thoughts and beliefs—Our ideas and beliefs greatly affect our emotions and actions. Develop positive ideas and beliefs about yourself, others and the world around you. Challenge negative and limiting beliefs and make improvements to make them positive and empowered. Practice positive self-dialogue and affirmations and surround yourself with positive influences. By developing positive ideas and beliefs, your intellect can be transformed towards joy and happiness.

Practice humour and playfulness—Humour and playfulness are powerful tools for creating joy and happiness. Explore moments of laughter and play in your daily life. Remain engaged in those activities that make you laugh, spend time with people who bring happiness and laughter into your life, and do not take yourself too seriously. Include humour and playfulness in your routine and watch your level of joy and happiness increase.

Create a sense of gratitude towards yourself—Creating a sense of gratitude towards yourself is as important as practising gratitude towards others. Accept your strengths, accomplishments and efforts as well as appreciate yourself for who you are. Avoid self-criticism and self-judgement and instead, practice self-praise and self-love. When you have a positive relationship with yourself, you are more likely to experience joy and happiness.

Examples of happiness and creating happiness

Kavita is a busy working professional who often finds herself caught up in the stress and demands of her job. She decided to include consciousness in her routine. She starts her day with a short meditation and takes a few moments in the entire day to pause, take a deep breath, and bring her focus to the present moment. She also practices gratitude by keeping a diary and writing down three things every day for which she is grateful. With time, Kavita noticed that she is more present, less stressed, and experiences more moments of joy and happiness in her daily life.

Jeevan is a retired person who has struggled with a sense of purpose and fulfilment after retiring from his long-time job. He decided to set meaningful goals for himself, such as voluntarily working in a local charity and adopting a new hobby. He also made efforts to reconnect with old friends and spend quality time with his family. As he pursued these meaningful activities, he gained a sense of purpose and joy afresh in his life, and there was a remarkable increase in his overall happiness.

Seema is a young professional who was constantly comparing herself to others and caught up in negative self-discussion. She decided to practice self-compassion and self-care by being kind to herself and practising positive self-dialogue. She also tried to participate in those activities that gave her happiness, such as painting, dancing and spending time with loved ones. Seema also made a conscious effort to disengage herself from social media for a few hours every day and instead, focused on remaining completely present in the current moment. As a result, she saw a remarkable increase in her level of joy and happiness, and her self-respect and self-worth increased.

Surendra is a middle-aged man who struggles with stress and anxiety due to work and family responsibilities. He decided to prioritise self-care and began a regular exercise schedule which he enjoyed, such as a long walking tour and cycling. He also made changes in his diet, incorporated more whole foods, and reduced his intake of processed foods. Apart from this, Surendra practiced consciousness and meditation to manage his stress level and create a sense of peace and joy. As he gave priority to his physical and intellectual well-being, he found that his overall happiness and satisfaction increased, and he was able to manage the challenges in his life in a better way.

Finally, the development of joy and happiness is a lifelong journey that requires active effort and practice. This is about adopting an intellect and lifestyle that prioritises welfare, self-care and positivity. By incorporating the above-mentioned examples, such as practising consciousness, setting meaningful goals, nurturing relationships, practising gratitude, taking care of physical and intellectual health, disengaging from technology, and adopting joy and playfulness, you can create joy and happiness in your life.

Remember, creating joy and happiness is unique for each person, and it may require experimentation and self-reflection to find what works best for you. It is important to be deliberate and consistent in your efforts to prioritise joy and happiness in your daily life. As you create joy and happiness, you will experience many benefits which include better intellectual and physical health, better relationships, an increase in resilience, and a great sense of fulfilment and purpose. Therefore, take responsibility for your own happiness and start creating joy in your life today.

❑

39

Enhancing Intuition and Self-inspiration

Intuition, which is often referred to as 'self-inspiration', is a powerful and simple cognitive process that permits us to make simple decisions quickly and spontaneously based on the stored knowledge and experiences of our subconscious mind. This is the 'inner feeling' or 'self-inspiration' that guides us, sometimes without any logical explanation. In this chapter, we shall explore the concept of intuition, its importance in making decisions, and how we can enhance our intuition and self-inspiration to become masters of our minds.

Understanding intuition

Intuition is a form of knowing, which is not based on conscious logic or logical explanation. This a process of making decisions easily, automatically and quickly which draws on our inner knowledge, feelings and experiences. This is often described as a 'self-inspiration' or 'sixth sense' which guides us in making decisions without fully understanding why or how.

Intuition operates on many levels which include emotional, physical and cognitive levels. Intuition is often emotionally associated with a feeling of resonance or restlessness. This shows that something seems right or wrong. Intuition can manifest physically in the form of physical sensations, such as stomach cramps, tingling or sensation. Intuition can manifest cognitively as a feeling of sudden insight, creative ideas, or a feeling of clarity about any situation or decision.

Intuition can be seen as a combination of our previous experiences, emotions and inner knowledge which are stored in our subconscious mind. These accumulated experiences and knowledge work as valuable resources, which can guide us in the present moment.

The importance of intuition in making decisions

Intuition plays an important role in making decisions because it can provide us with valuable insight and guidance while facing complex situations or making difficult choices. While our conscious mind depends on logic and logical explanation, our intuition can tap the vast knowledge and experiences of the subconscious mind to provide a unique perspective and solution.

Intuition can be especially helpful in those situations where time is limited and we need to make quick decisions. For example, a doctor can rely on his intuition while treating an asymptomatic patient, or a business leader can use his intuition to make strategic decisions in a rapidly changing market.

Intuition can also complement our rational decision-making process. This can work as an additional source of information and help us evaluate and verify our conscious decisions. When our intuition conforms with our logical reasoning, it can provide us with self-confidence and assurance in our choices.

Examples of enhancing intuition and self-inspiration

Enhancing our intuition and self-inspiration can be a valuable skill because it can help us make better decisions, improve our decisions, and become more self-aware. Some examples have been given here of how we can enhance our intuition and self-inspiration.

Creating consciousness—Consciousness is the conscious state of the current moment. Practising consciousness can help us calm our fast-paced thoughts, reduce distractions, and attune us to our inner knowledge and intuition.

For example, let us consider a woman, Sara, who wants to enhance her intuition in making career-related decisions. Sara practices consciousness by fixing a regular time for meditation and reflection. During these moments of consciousness, she focuses on her ideas, feelings and physical sensations without judgement or attachment.

Sara practices consciousness in her daily activities as well, such as listening to the signals of her body, being completely present in conversations, and observing her environment without judgement. Sara develops a deep relationship with herself through consciousness, enhances her intuition, and becomes more accustomed to her intuitive feelings in making decisions related to her career.

Respecting feelings—Our feelings can provide valuable clues and insight into our intuition and self-inspiration. By respecting our feelings and heeding them without judgement or repression, we can tap our intuition or self-inspiration more effectively.

For example, let us assume that you are considering a job offer, which looks good on paper but you are feeling restless. Instead of eliminating the feeling or rationalising it, you can choose to respect it and explore it further. Take some time to consider the source of inconvenience and what your emotions are trying to tell you. It may be possible that your intuition is picking up on something that your logical mind has missed, such as misalignment with your values or possible danger.

Reflect on previous experiences—Our previous experiences are valuable resources that can inform our intuition and self-inspiration. By reflecting on our previous successes, failures, and lessons learnt, we can get help in drawing on that accumulated knowledge and science in the current time.

For example, imagine that you are facing a challenging situation at work, for which, a decision with possible risks and benefits is required. Considering similar situations faced by you in the past and how you navigated them can provide insight and guidance for the present situation. Your intuition can draw on those previous experiences to guide you in making the correct decision.

Trusting the process—In order to trust our intuition and self-inspiration, it is essential to control and trust the process. This means being open to receiving insight and guidance without understanding or knowing the logical reasoning behind it.

For example, let us assume that you are in a brainstorming session with your team and you have an idea that comes suddenly and strongly to you. It is possible that you are not able to explain why you had this thought. However, you can choose to trust it and share it with the team. This can prove to be a great solution which you cannot reach by logical explanation only.

Make place for intuition—It is necessary to make place for intuition in our busy and fast-paced life. This means permitting yourself to slow down, calm your mind, and create opportunities for reflection and introspection.

For example, you can take a walk in nature regularly for calm reflection, journaling or just to make place for your intuition. Giving yourself time and space to disconnect from technology, reducing distractions, and listening to your inner knowledge can help enhance your intuition and self-inspiration.

Finally, enhancing intuition and self-inspiration is a valuable skill that can help us make better decisions, make improvements in our decisions, and become more aware of ourselves. By developing consciousness, respecting our feelings, reflecting on previous experiences, trusting the process, and making place for intuition, we can exploit our intuition and choose options that align with our authentic selves.

It is important to remember that intuition is not infallible and should not be the only basis for making a decision. It should be used in combination with our rational mind and critical thinking skills. However, by developing our intuition as well as trusting it, we can reach a valuable source of guidance and knowledge, which can help us navigate the complexities of life.

Remember, you have the power to be a master of your own mind, and enhancing your intuition and self-inspiration can be a powerful tool in the journey of your personal development and self-mastery.

❑

40

Fostering Healthy Habits

Habits play an important role in our lives. They are automatic behaviour and routine which shape our days and affect our overall welfare. From brushing our teeth in the morning to scrolling social media before sleeping, habits can affect our physical health, intellectual welfare, and emotional state. Therefore, it is important to develop healthy habits in our journey of becoming masters of our minds. In this chapter, we shall explore the importance of fostering healthy habits and provide examples of how to develop and maintain them.

Understanding habits

Habits are deeply inherent patterns in behaviour formed by strengthening and repetition. They are formed in the 'basal ganglia', the part of the brain responsible for habit formation and automatic behaviour. When we repeat any behaviour in a relevant context, our mind forms a neural pathway that makes behaviour more automatic and less dependent on conscious effort.

Habits may be either positive or negative. This depends on those behaviours which we engage in, again and again. For example, habits such as regular exercise, practice of consciousness, and healthy food can be positive and contribute to our overall welfare. On the other hand, habits such as excessive screen time, procrastination, or unhealthy food can be harmful to our physical and intellectual health.

Fostering healthy habits

Deliberate effort and consistency are required to foster healthy habits. Some examples have been given here of how you can develop and maintain healthy habits:

Make a small beginning—It is important to start small while fostering healthy habits. An attempt to make too many changes at once can be tiring and unstable. Instead of this, focus on one habit at a time and break it down into small, manageable steps.

For example, if you want to develop the habit of regular exercise, start with a small goal, such as taking a ten-minute walk thrice a week. Once this becomes a compatible part of your life, you can slowly increase the duration or frequency of your exercise sessions.

Set clear and specific goals—Setting clear and specific goals helps you focus on your desired habit. Unclear goals such as 'exercise more' or 'eat nutritious food' are less effective as compared to specific goals such as 'jog for thirty minutes every Monday, Wednesday and Friday' or 'eat at least one green vegetable with each meal'.

A clear and specific goal gives you a clear direction, and it is easy to measure your progress. It also permits you to track your success and adjust it as necessary.

Prepare a plan—It is essential to prepare a plan in order to establish healthy habits. A plan helps you prepare an outline of the steps that you need to take, the resources you need, and the possible challenges you may have to face.

For example, if you want to form a habit of daily meditation, you can prepare a plan that includes setting a specific time each day, finding a peaceful and comfortable place, and using a meditation app or other resources to guide your practice. A plan can help you remain on track and overcome upcoming challenges.

Make it convenient—Convenience is an important factor in forming a habit. If a lot of effort or facilities are required for any habit, it is less likely to persist. Therefore, it is important to make healthy habits as convenient as possible.

For example, if you want to develop the habit of drinking more water throughout the day, you can keep a bottle of water with you all the time, set a reminder on your phone, or keep a jug of water on your desk or countertop. You can increase the possibility of forming this habit by making it easy to include it in your desired behaviour.

Create accountability—Accountability can be a powerful factor for habit formation. By sharing your goals and progress with others, you can create a sense of external accountability that can help you remain committed to your healthy habits.

For example, you can join an exercise group, or a challenge for healthy eating, or find an answerable partner, who shares the same goals. You can also track your progress in a journal or app and regularly review your successes as well as challenges and reflect on them. Creating accountability in the process of forming your habit can help you remain inspired and on track, even if it is difficult to move forward.

Change unhealthy habits with healthy ones—It can be challenging to break unhealthy habits but the process can be easier by changing them with healthy choices. Identify triggers or signals that inspire your unhealthy habits and explore healthy options to change them.

For example, if you snack on unhealthy food products when stressed, you can change this habit with a healthy coping tool, such as walking, practising deep breathing, or talking with a friend. By changing unhealthy habits with healthy ones, not only do you break the cycle of negative behaviours, but also, establish new, positive habits in their place.

Remain consistent and patient—It takes time and hard work to form healthy habits and it is important to remain consistent as well as patient during the entire process. It is normal to face failures, slips and challenges along the way. However, it is essential that you remain committed to your goals and not give up easily.

Remember, habits are formed by repetition and it takes time for new behaviours to become automatic. Be kind to yourself, practice self-compassion, and celebrate small victories on the way. Be consistent, patient and committed to your healthy habits and eventually, they will become second nature.

Examples of healthy habits

Let us now examine some examples of healthy habits that you can include in your routine:

Regular exercise—Exercise is important to maintain physical health and fitness. There can be many benefits of forming a habit of regular exercise including better heart health, increased strength and resilience, better mood, and less stress.

You can start with simple activities such as walking for thirty minutes every day, three to five days a week, jogging or cycling. You can also explore different forms of exercise based on your interests and fitness level, such as swimming, yoga or strength training. Explore what is best for you and make it a compatible part of your routine.

Mindful eating—Mindful eating is a healthy habit that involves focusing on the taste, smell, texture and joy of food, without being distracted. This helps you develop a healthy relationship with food and stops you from eating mindlessly, which can prevent over-eating and malnutrition.

You can practice careful eating by eating slowly, tasting each morsel, and focusing on the signals of hunger as well as fullness. Avoid distracted eating, such as while watching TV or working on your computer, because this can form the habit of mindless eating.

Instead, prepare a peaceful and happy environment for your meal and remain fully present during the experience of eating.

Sufficient sleep—Sleep is essential for overall health and strength. Forming habits of healthy sleep can improve your mood, cognitive functions, immune system, and overall quality of life.

Prepare a consistent sleep schedule by going to bed and waking up at the same time every day, even on weekends. Establish a peaceful sleep routine, such as reading a book, taking a warm bath, or practising relaxation techniques, to send signals to your body that this is the time to relax. Avoid stimulating techniques such as using electronic gadgets or drinking caffeine at bedtime, because this can disrupt your sleep.

Daily meditation or practice of consciousness—Meditation or practising consciousness is a healthy habit that can improve your intellectual well-being, reduce stress, and increase self-consciousness. This involves focusing on the current moment without judgement.

You can start with a few minutes only of meditation or mindful practice every day and increase the duration slowly as you become more comfortable. There are different types of meditation or mindful practices such as guided meditation, body scan, loving-kindness meditation, or just observing your breathing. Find a practice that resonates with you and make it a regular part of your routine, in order to gain benefits.

Hydration—It is essential to remain hydrated for overall health and strength. Drinking enough water during the day can help maintain proper body functions, support healthy digestion, promote clear skin, and prevent dehydration.

Form a habit of drinking water regularly throughout the day and take a bottle of water with you to ensure its easy availability. You can also add fruits, vegetables and herbs to the water to enhance its taste and make it more enjoyable to drink. Avoid sugary drinks or excessive caffeine because they can dehydrate your body.

The practice of gratitude—Practising gratitude is a healthy habit that can improve your intellectual well-being and overall perspective of life. It includes deliberately focusing on the positive aspects of your life and expressing gratitude for them.

You can start by keeping a gratitude diary and writing three things every day for which you are grateful. You can also express gratitude orally or intellectually and practice mindfulness to fully appreciate the present moment. In order to develop a positive intellect, include gratitude in your routine, during morning or evening rituals.

Daily momentum—Regular momentum throughout the day is essential to maintain good physical health. Sitting for long durations can negatively impact your posture, metabolism and overall health. Developing a habit of daily activity can improve your physical fitness, energy levels, and overall welfare.

Include activities in your daily routine, such as taking a short walk, doing stretches or squats, or simple lung exercises. You can also explore different physical activities that you enjoy, such as dancing, playing a sport, or taking a fitness class. Find ways to make activity a natural part of your day, even if you have a sedentary job.

Limiting screen time—In today's digital age, excessive screen time can hurt your intellectual and physical health. Spending excessive time at the screen can lead to eye strain, poor sleep, sluggish behaviour, and social isolation.

Develop healthy habits around screen time by setting limits on the usage of your devices. Set aside screen-free time, such as during meals or one hour before sleeping, so that you can disconnect yourself and focus on other activities. You can also participate in screen-free hobbies or activities to reduce your total screen time, such as reading books, spending time with nature, or pursuing hobbies.

Prioritising self-care— Taking care of yourself is essential for maintaining good intellectual health and strength. This includes acting deliberately to take care of your physical, intellectual and emotional needs.

Include self-care as an essential part of your routine by prioritising activities that nurture your body, mind and soul. This may include getting enough sleep, eating nutritious food, taking a break when needed, practising relaxation techniques, participating in hobbies, spending time with loved ones, and seeking professional help when required. By prioritising self-care, you will gain help in recharging, reducing stress, and improving your overall well-being.

Fostering positive relationships—Positive relationships are important for our intellectual and emotional welfare. Surrounding yourself with helpful, positive and similar thinking people can have a significant impact on your happiness and overall quality of life.

Make it a habit to develop and maintain positive relationships in your life. This can include spending time with loved ones, reaching out to friends or family members, joining social or community groups, volunteering or obtaining professional help when required. Nurturing positive relationships will help you feel connected, supported and emotionally fulfilled.

Forming healthy habits is essential for improving your overall welfare and empowering yourself to become a master of your mind. You can exert a positive influence on your physical, intellectual and emotional health by consciously including healthy habits in your routine and eventually, improve the quality of your life.

Keep in mind that developing healthy habits takes time and hard work. It is important to be patient with yourself and permit some flexibility because you work in the direction of establishing a new routine. Start small, focus on one habit at a time, and slowly act on it. Consistency is important. Therefore, set a goal of practising these habits regularly till they become second nature.

Apart from this, it is important to align your healthy habits according to your specific requirements and lifestyle. What works for one person may not work for another. Therefore, it is necessary to listen to your body and mind and adjust accordingly. Beware of your own limitations and prioritise self-care throughout the entire process.

Remember that habits are formed by repetition and consistency. It may take time and effort to develop healthy habits but its long-term benefits are certain. Through firm resolve, self-awareness and deliberate effort, you can form healthy habits that support your physical, intellectual and emotional welfare and empower you to become a master of your own mind.

Finally, forming healthy habits is a powerful tool to control your mind and improve your overall welfare. This requires self-awareness, determination and consistent effort but its long-term benefits are inevitable. Develop healthy habits such as self-reflection, consciousness, regular exercise, healthy food, hydration, gratitude, daily activity, limiting screen time, prioritising self-care, creating positive relationships in your life and observing yourself intellectually as well as emotionally. Remember, you have the power to form healthy habits that can transform your life and empower you to become a master of your own mind. Take the first step today and begin developing healthy habits that will aid your well-being in the years to come.

❑

41

Mastering the Art of Meditation

Meditation is a powerful instrument that has been used for centuries to develop a calm and focused mind, reduce stress, improve intellectual clarity, and enhance overall well-being. This is an ancient method that has withstood the test of time and is widely recognised for its many benefits for the mind, body and soul. In this chapter, we shall explore the art of meditation, its different forms and techniques, and also learn how to master it by making it a valuable tool in the journey of becoming masters of our minds.

Understanding meditation

Meditation is an exercise that involves training the mind for deep rest, focus and enhancement of consciousness. It is often connected to consciousness which is the practice of focusing on the current moment without judgement. Although meditation is rooted in ancient spiritual and religious traditions, it has developed to become a secular practice that is accessible to people of all backgrounds and beliefs.

Meditation is not about emptying the mind or attaining a state of complete silence; rather, it is about developing the quality of consciousness that permits us to observe our thoughts, feelings and sensations, without getting trapped in them. It is a practice that creates a sense of detachment from our thoughts and helps us develop a non-reactive and non-judgemental attitude towards them.

Benefits of meditation

The practice of meditation has been scientifically proven to be widely beneficial for intellectual, emotional and physical welfare. Some chief benefits of meditation include:

Less stress and anxiety—Meditation has been shown to activate the body's relaxation response which helps in reducing the production of the stress hormone and blood pressure. Practising regular meditation can help people manage stress and anxiety more effectively.

Better intellectual clarity and focus—Meditation helps improve concentration and focus by training the mind to remain in the present and avoid distractions. It can enhance cognitive functions as well as improve memory and attention span.

Increase in self-consciousness—Meditation creates self-consciousness by which a person becomes more habitual of his ideas, emotions and sensations. This increased self-consciousness can lead to better emotional regulation, better decisions, and enhanced self-reflection.

Enhanced emotional well-being—Meditation can improve emotional flexibility and regulation by helping people develop a greater sense of equanimity and calm to face challenges. It can also promote positive emotions such as kindness, compassion and gratitude.

Better physical health—Meditation has a positive impact on physical health which includes less inflammation, better immune functions, and reduced risk of chronic ailments such as heart disease and diabetes.

Enhanced creativity and intuition—Meditation can help people tap into their inner creativity and intuition by calming the mind and permitting deep insight as well as inspiration to emerge.

Mastering the art of meditation

Meditation is a skill that can be developed through regular practice and dedication. Some main principles and techniques are given here that can help people master the art of meditation:

Start from basic facts—If you are new to meditation, it is important to start from basic facts. Find a calm and comfortable place for sitting or lying down where you will not be disturbed. Close your eyes and take a few deep breaths to relax your body and mind. Start with short sessions such as 5-10 minutes and slowly increase the duration, as you become more comfortable with practice.

Choose a meditation technique—There are different forms of meditation. Choose one that resonates with you. Some general forms of meditation include consciousness meditation, loving-kindness meditation, body scan meditation, and breath awareness meditation. Experiment with different techniques and find the one that you like best.

Focus on your breathing—Focusing on your breathing is one of the most common techniques used in meditation. Focus on the sensation of your breath as it goes in and out through your nose and chest. Focus on the rhythm (flow), temperature and the sensation of each breath, without trying to change it. When your mind wanders here and there, bring your focus back slowly to your breaths, without judgement or frustration.

Create consciousness—Consciousness is the practice of focusing on the current moment without judgement. It involves being fully present and aware of your thoughts, feelings, sensations and the environment around you. Develop consciousness without engaging in or trying to change whatever arises in your experience as you meditate. Permit things to come and go and whenever your mind wanders, bring your focus back to the current moment.

Practice loving-kindness—Loving-kindness meditation which is also known as 'metta' meditation, involves creating a feeling of love and kindness towards yourself and others. Start by directing loving-kindness towards yourself, then extend it to loved ones, acquaintances, strangers and also those people with whom you may have problems. Use phrases such as, 'Can I be happy?', 'Can I remain healthy?', 'Can I remain safe?' or 'Can I be comfortable?' and repeat them either silently or loudly, because you send good wishes to yourself and others.

Develop patience and consistency—Meditation is a practice that requires patience and consistency. It is not something that can be gained overnight and sometimes, progress can be slow. Be patient with yourself and avoid believing your meditation sessions to be 'good' or 'bad'. Whatever emerges in your practice, inspect and accept it without attachment or hatred. Consistency is also important. Therefore, try to establish a regular routine of meditation and make it a habit in your daily life.

Include meditation in your daily life—Meditation is not something to be done only during formal practice; rather, it can be incorporated into your daily life as well. Practice awareness and consciousness when you think about your daily activities, such as eating, walking or talking to others. Include the benefits of meditation in your routine, such as presence, non-judgement, kindness in your conversation with others and a way of living a conscious and active life.

Examples of meditation in daily life

Meditation can be practiced in different ways in your daily life. Some examples of how you can include meditation in your routine are given here:

Morning meditation—Start your day with a short session of meditation so that the tone can be set for the day. Find a peaceful place, sit comfortably, and practice your chosen technique of meditation for a few minutes. This can help you start your day with a calm and focused mind and set a positive tone for the rest of your day.

Mindful eating—Practice consciousness while eating meals. Focus on the taste, texture and smell of your food. Chew slowly and taste each morsel. Focus and when your mind wanders to different things, slowly bring your focus back to your food. This can help you develop consciousness and healthy eating habits as well as be more appreciative of your food.

Walking meditation—Change your daily walk into a meditation practice. Focus on the feeling of your feet against the ground, the momentum of your body, and the sounds and images around you. Let yourself experience the complete act of walking, without losing yourself in thoughts or distractions.

Mindful communication—Practice meditation while talking to others. Listen completely to the person to whom you are talking, without any interruption or thinking about what you are going to reply. While communicating, focus on your reactions, feelings as well as thoughts, and give your response with kindness and compassion. This can help you improve your communication skills, deepen your bonds with others as well as develop a more considerate and kind way of relating to others.

Bedtime meditation—End your day with a meditation session before going to sleep in order to relax your mind and body. Lie down comfortably on the bed and practice relaxation techniques or guided meditation, to eliminate the stress and anxieties of the entire day. This can help you sleep comfortably at night and feel refreshed in the morning.

Brain work—Be careful in your work by taking short breaks throughout the day to practice meditation or just to remain present in the current moment. Focus on your breathing and the sensations of your body, and consider your thoughts as well as feelings, without getting trapped in them. This can help you reduce stress, focus and increase productivity as well as create an enhanced mental perspective for work.

Mindful household chores—Change household chores into a meditation practice. Focus completely on the work whether it is washing utensils and clothes or cleaning your house. Focus on the sensations, bustle and smells associated with the work and let go of any emerging thought or distraction. This can help you create consciousness in everyday activities and change them into opportunities for meditation.

Nature meditation—Spend time in nature and use this in the form of a meditation practice. Go for a walk in the park, sit by the seashore, or go on a long, walking tour in the mountains. Focus on the scenes, sounds and smell of nature and allow yourself to be fully present in the moment. This can help you connect with the natural world, reduce stress, and create a feeling of astonishment and praise for the beauty around you.

Compassionate meditation—Practice compassionate meditation by sending good wishes to yourself and others. Sit comfortably and repeat phrases silently, such as, 'May all people be happy', 'May all people be healthy', and 'May all people be safe'. Include yourself, loved ones, acquaintances, strangers and even those with whom you may have problems. This can help you create compassion, sympathy, and a feeling of mutual association with all people.

Finally, meditation is a powerful tool in the art of mastering your brain. This can help you develop inner strength, manage stress, enhance self-consciousness, and develop a more considerate and kind way of living life. By practising meditation regularly and including it in your daily life, you can become a master of your own mind and live a more balanced, peaceful and complete life.

Remember, meditation is a practice, and progress can be made slowly. Be patient with yourself and practice your meditation with curiosity, openness and a non-judgemental approach. Experiment with different techniques, explore what is best for you, and make it a part of your routine. With time and consistency, you can develop a strong meditation practice that supports your intellectual, emotional and physical welfare as well as helps you navigate the challenges of life with more ease and flexibility.

Therefore, take a deep breath, sit comfortably and begin the journey of mastering the art of meditation. Discover inner peace, clarity and knowledge that is inside you as well as unlock the full potential of your mind. You have the power to change your mind, and meditation can be your guide on this beautiful journey of self-discovery and self-mastery.

❑

42

Sleep and Rest

Sleep is an essential aspect of our physical and intellectual welfare. It plays a significant role in our overall health, cognitive functions, emotional regulation, and daily performance. However, many people struggle with sleep problems in today's fast-paced world, such as difficulty in sleeping, consistent sleep, or restful sleep. In this chapter, we shall explore different strategies and examples to improve sleep and rest, so that we can make our lives successful.

Understanding the importance of sleep

Sleep is not only a passive state of unconsciousness; it is an active process that plays an important role in our physical and intellectual health. During sleep, our body goes through many important processes, such as the repair of tissues, hormone regulation, and memory consolidation. Why is sleep important? Some major reasons for the same have been given here:

Restoration of the body—Sleep permits the body to repair and restore itself. The body produces development hormone during sleep which helps in tissue repair, cell rejuvenation, and the functioning of the immune system. It also helps in regulating metabolism, blood sugar levels, and heart health.

Enhancing cognitive functions—Sleep plays an important role in cognitive processes such as learning, memory consolidation, problem-solving and creativity. It helps in brain processes and organises information which is essential for optimal cognitive performance during waking hours.

Emotional regulation—Sleep is closely associated with emotional welfare. Getting sufficient sleep is essential for emotional regulation, mood stability, and stress management. Lack of sleep can increase irritability, temper and emotional reactions.

Physical performance—Sleep is essential for strength, patience, coordination, balance and physical performance. Athletes, especially, require sufficient sleep for optimal performance and recovery.

Overall health—Chronic insomnia can be connected to different health problems, such as obesity, diabetes, heart disease, weak immune system, and intellectual health disorders. It is essential to get sufficient, quality sleep for overall health and fitness.

Come, let us now explore some strategies and examples to improve sleep and rest so that you can control your mind.

Creating a conducive environment for sleep

The environment in which you sleep plays a significant role in the quality of your sleep. Some strategies and examples to create an environment conducive to sleep have been given below:

Keep your bedroom dark—Ensure that there is darkness in your bedroom while sleeping. Use black curtains to block any outside light and consider removing any electronic gadget with a shiny screen that can disrupt your circadian rhythms.

Maintain a comfortable temperature— Keep your bedroom at a cool, comfortable temperature that is conducive to sleep. Avoid excessive heat or cold because it can disrupt your sleep.

Reduce noise—Reduce noise in your bedroom by using earplugs, noise cancelling machines or soundproofing. Noise can disrupt your sleep and affect its quality.

Comfortable mattresses and pillows—Comfortable mattresses and pillows are important for good sleep. Choose a mattress and pillow that support your body and sleep preferences. Change them when they go bad or become uncomfortable.

Organise your bedroom—Keep your bedroom clean and organised in order to create a relaxing and peaceful environment. Clutter can create visual distractions and affect the quality of your sleep.

Establishing a consistent sleep routine

A regular sleep routine can help in regulating your body's inner clock and improving the quality of your sleep. Some strategies and examples through which a consistent sleep routine can be established are given here:

Set a regular bedtime—Try to sleep and wake up at the same time every day, including weekends. This helps regulate your circadian rhythms and enhances better quality of sleep.

Set a bedtime—Establish a comfortable sleep routine to signal your body that this is the time to rest and get ready for sleep. It can include activities such as reading, listening to soothing music, practising relaxation techniques, or taking a warm bath.

Limit screen time before sleeping—The light from electronic gadgets such as smartphones, tablets and computers can block the production of melatonin, the sleep-regulating hormone. Limit your screen time at least one hour before sleeping, in order to promote better sleep.

Avoid stimulating activities before sleeping—Engaging in stimulating activities such as intense exercise, work-related tasks, or tense discussions close to bedtime, can make it difficult for your body and mind to rest. Try to avoid such activities before bedtime in order to relax your body and prepare it for rest.

Create a peaceful environment at bedtime—Make your bedtime environment peaceful and comfortable. This can include dimming the lights, using relaxing scents such as lavender as well as creating a comfortable sleep environment with a comfortable blanket and pillow.

Managing lifestyle factors for better sleep

Many lifestyle factors can affect the quality of your sleep. You can improve your sleep and rest by making healthy lifestyle choices. Some strategies and examples have been given here:

Regular exercise—Regular physical activity during the day can help in improving the quality of your sleep. However, avoid intense exercise near bedtime because this can have the opposite effect and can stimulate your body.

Balanced diet—Eating a healthy, balanced diet can also affect the quality of your sleep. Avoid heavy food, caffeine and alcohol before sleeping because they can disrupt your sleep. Instead, choose light, nutritious food and limit your intake of stimulating products.

Manage stress—High-level stress can disrupt your sleep. Practice stress management techniques such as relaxation practice, consciousness, or consulting a doctor, in order to manage stress effectively and improve your sleep.

Prepare a peaceful sleep routine—Establishing a peaceful sleep routine can help you rest and get ready for sleep. This may include activities such as reading, listening to soothing music, or engaging in relaxation techniques.

Limit naps—Whereas taking naps can be beneficial for some people, taking excessive naps during the day can disrupt your sleep at night. Nap for only 20-30 minutes during the day, in order to avoid disrupting your sleep at night.

Limit your intake of alcohol and caffeine—Alcohol and caffeine are known to disrupt sleep. Limit the intake of these products to improve the quality of your sleep, especially near bedtime.

Practice relaxation techniques for better sleep

Relaxation techniques can help calm your mind as well as your body and can promote better sleep. Some relaxation techniques that you can practice are given here:

Taking deep breaths—Taking deep breaths is a simple relaxation technique that can help in calming your mind and body. Lie down comfortably, take a slow, deep breath through your nose, and release through your mouth. Focus on your breathing and let yourself relax.

Progressive muscle relaxation—Progressive muscle relaxation involves tensing and relaxing different muscle groups of your body in order to release stress and promote relaxation. Lie down comfortably and begin with the tensing and relaxing of the fingers of your feet, then move upwards to your feet, thighs, stomach, chest, arms, etc., till you reach your head.

Guided imagery—Guided imagery involves using your imagination to create soothing intellectual images. You can listen to pre-recorded guided imagery sources or create one of your own. Imagine yourself in a peaceful, calm environment, such as the seashore, forest or meadow; let yourself relax and release any stress.

Meditation—Meditation is a powerful relaxation technique that can help in relaxing your mind and body as well as promoting better sleep. There are different types of meditation, such as mindful meditation, loving-kindness meditation, and body scan meditation that you can practice for relaxing as well as preparing for sleep.

Yoga—Yoga is a gentle form of exercise that connects physical momentum with meditation as well as relaxation techniques, through which it becomes an excellent exercise for improving sleep and rest. Some yoga poses such as 'bal mudra' (child pose), leg-up-the-wall pose and 'shavasan' can help in relaxing your body and calming your mind as well as promoting better sleep.

Aromatherapy—Using calming scents such as lavender, chamomile or bergamot through aromatherapy, can help promote better sleep and relax your mind and body. You can use essential oils in a diffuser, spray them on your pillow, or add them to a warm bath in order to create a peaceful sleep environment.

Better sleep—Practising better sleep habits can greatly impact the quality of your sleep. This includes establishing a consistent sleep schedule, keeping your bedroom dark, peaceful and at a comfortable temperature as well as using your bed for sleep and intimacy only.

Cognitive behaviour therapy for sleeplessness—This is a kind of therapy that is focused on identifying as well as changing negative thought patterns and behaviour associated with sleep. It is extremely effective in improving the quality of sleep and is often used as a first-line treatment for sleeplessness.

Real-life examples of improving sleep and relaxation

Come, let us consider some real-life examples of how people have successfully improved their sleep and relaxation:

Seema, a working professional in her mid-thirties, would struggle to sleep all night. She decided to create a peaceful sleep routine which included reading a book, practising deep breathing, and using lavender in a diffuser. She established a consistent sleep schedule as well, limited her intake of caffeine, and avoided screen time before sleep. With these changes, Seema noticed a significant improvement in the quality of her sleep and felt more refreshed and energetic during the day.

Manoj, a college student in his early twenties, followed an irregular sleep pattern due to studying till late in the night as well as napping often during the day. He decided to prioritise his sleep, established a consistent sleep schedule, and limited his nap to twenty minutes during the day. He decided not to exercise before sleeping in order to help himself relax as well as unwind and practiced meditation as well. As a result, the quality of his sleep improved, and he found himself to be more alert and focused during his classes.

Lata, a stay-at-home woman in her late forties, struggled with baseless thoughts and anxieties at night which affected her ability to sleep. She decided to practice consciousness meditation and guided imagery before sleeping, in order to calm her mind and relax her body. She created a peaceful sleep environment as well, by using dim lights, playing soft music, and avoiding the screen before sleeping. With these changes, Lata observed a remarkable decrease in her night anxieties, and the quality of her sleep improved.

Finally, improvement in sleep and rest is important for overall welfare and intellectual health. You can improve the quality of your sleep effectively as well as feel refreshed and rejuvenated by including healthy sleep habits, managing lifestyle factors, and practising relaxation techniques. Remember, everyone's sleep requirements are different. Therefore, it is important to know what is best for you. Prioritise it in your routine. With constant effort and practice, you can become a master of your own mind and get restful sleep.

❑

43

Mastering the Art of Letting Go

One of the most essential skills for controlling your mind is the ability to let go. Letting go is liberating yourself from the attachment of those ideas, feelings, beliefs and situations that are now useless for you. This requires the desire to release control, surrender to the current moment, and let life flow without resistance. Mastering the art of letting go can lead to more peace, freedom and welfare. In this chapter, we shall explore the concept of letting go and understand why it is so important for intellectual mastery. We shall also provide examples of how you can develop the skill of letting go in your daily life.

Understanding the concept of letting go

Letting go is not about accepting defeat or being passive. It is about releasing the grip of attachment, releasing resistance, and letting life unfold naturally. It is about recognising that some things are out of your control and holding on to them only causes suffering. Letting go is a process of surrender and acceptance, without judgement or resistance. It involves releasing those ideas, feelings, beliefs and situations that are not serving you now and making place for new experiences, perspectives and possibilities.

Letting go does not mean forgetting the past or ignoring it nor does it mean neglecting the future. It means being fully present in this moment and permitting yourself to experience the flow of life, without holding on to the past or understanding the future. It means being aware of your emotions and thoughts and letting them move on without holding on to them. It means releasing the necessity of control and believing that life will unfurl naturally.

Why is letting go important for intellectual mastery?

Letting go is an important skill for intellectual mastery because it permits you to liberate yourself from the bonds of the past, anxieties of the future, and the limitations of your thoughts and beliefs. When you hold on tightly to those ideas, feelings, beliefs and situations that do not serve you now, you create unnecessary pain and resistance in your mind. This can cause intellectual and emotional problems as well as hinder your ability to react effectively in the present moment.

Letting go enables you to release your intellectual and emotional burden, which lightens you and makes way for new perspectives, insights and possibilities. This permits you to move forward with more clarity and flexibility. Letting go promotes self-consciousness as well because, for this, you need to be aware of your thoughts, feelings and attachments. This self-consciousness permits you to develop a healthy relationship with your mind and make conscious choices, instead of being inspired by the subconscious pattern of ideas and behaviour.

Examples of letting go in everyday life

Letting go is an exercise that can be applied to various aspects of life. Some examples of how you can develop the skill of letting go in your daily life have been given here:

Letting go of past regrets

Situation—You are troubled by regrets, mistakes or failures of the past which keep affecting your mood and health.

Letting go (let go) response—By accepting the regrets of the past without judgement, and accepting the fact that you cannot change the past. Recognise that regrets only keep the pain in the present moment. Instead of this, focus on the present moment and what you can do now to bring about a positive change. Practice self-forgiveness and self-compassion by granting yourself kindness and understanding. Remain engaged in activities that give you happiness and satisfaction in the current moment and let go off the necessity to focus on the past.

Stop worrying about the future

Situation—You are constantly worried about the future, such as financial worries, health-related issues, or relationships, which cause anxiety and stress.

Letting go (let go) response—Practice not worrying about the future by recognising that worrying does not change results. It only adds unnecessary stress and anxiety to the current moment. Accept that the future is uncertain and you cannot control everything. Focus on what can you do in the current moment to prepare for the future, such as taking practical steps, making correct decisions, and believing in your ability to be able to deal with whatever comes your way. Instead of losing yourself in worries about the future, practice awareness and remain fully present in this moment. Create positive intelligence and belief in the inherent goodness of life.

Letting go of negative thoughts and beliefs

Situation—You are plagued by negative ideas, self-doubt, and limiting beliefs which hinder you from reaching your full potential.

Let go response—Without judging negative ideas and beliefs, practice being aware of them and letting go of them. Recognise that ideas are not facts and you have the power to choose which ideas are to be believed in and which are to be focused upon. Challenge negative ideas and beliefs by questioning their validity and changing them with positive, strong ones. Practice self-compassion and self-acceptance, and let go off the necessity to constantly evaluate and criticise yourself. Keep busy in positive self-dialogue as well as affirmations, and surround yourself with helpful people and environments that uplift you.

Giving up control

Situation—You have a strict need to control every aspect of your life, in which, the behaviour of others and external circumstances are included and these create stress and frustration.

Let go response—Practice giving up control by recognising that some things are out of your control and trying to control everything only leads to unnecessary stress and pain. Practice surrendering to the present moment and let life unfurl naturally. Believe in your abilities and knowledge of life. Focus on what you can control, such as your thoughts, emotions and actions, and let go of the necessity to control external circumstances or other people. Practice flexibility as well as compatibility, and embrace the unknown and uncertainties of life with an open mind and heart.

Renouncing attachment and hatred

Situation—You hold grudges and resentment towards others for past sorrows and injustices, which keeps you trapped in negative emotions and blocks healing and development.

Let go response—Practice accepting the feelings that arise and after accepting them, practice letting go of dissatisfaction as well as anger and then consciously choose to release them. Recognise the fact that holding on to hatred and resentment only perpetuates pain in your own mind and body. Practice forgiveness towards both yourself and others as a form of releasing yourself from the emotional burden of the past. Cultivate sympathy, kindness and understanding towards others, focus on healing, and move forward with an open heart and mind.

Giving up attachment to material possessions

Situation—You are attached to material possessions such as wealth, property or status, which create a sense of identity and security but also create greed, attachment and pain.

Let go response—Practice letting go of attachment to material objects by recognising that possessions do not define your values or happiness. Consider the impermanence of material possessions and the transient nature of material wealth and status. Instead of constantly trying for more, develop an intellect of abundance and gratitude for whatever you have in the present moment. Practice benevolence and asceticism by sharing your possessions with others and giving up the need to accumulate material wealth as the primary source of happiness. Focus on developing inner qualities such as love, compassion and knowledge, which bring permanent satisfaction and happiness.

Letting go of expectations

Situation—How should things be? Or how should others behave? You have rigid expectations about this which lead you towards disappointment, frustration and struggle, when reality does not meet your expectations.

Let go response—Practice letting go of expectations by recognising that expectations are often based on individual assumptions and assessments and that they cannot always align with reality. Be open to the possibility of different results and perspectives and let others be what they are, without imposing your expectations on them. Practice acceptance and compatibility and embrace the current moment in the same way, without making constant efforts to make things different. Focus on developing a flexible and open intellect and learn to let go of those rigid expectations, which can limit your ability to experience and appreciate life fully.

Examples of letting go in practice

Come, let us consider some practical examples of applying the art of letting go in different situations:

Letting go of an old relationship

Meena had gone through a difficult breakup with her long-term partner. She found herself in the past constantly, revisiting memories, and felt trapped in sadness and anger. She felt that holding on to the past was preventing her from moving forward and finding peace. Meena decided to practice letting go of her feelings while accepting them, permitted herself to mourn her loss, and actively chose to let go of her attachment to the past. She practiced self-compassion and forgiveness towards herself and her ex-partner and focused on the current moment and self-healing. Meena is engaged in self-care, spends time with helpful friends as well as family, and pursues new hobbies and interests. With time, Meena found that she was able to give up the past and open herself to new possibilities and a bright future.

Giving up perfectionism

Pravin was always a perfectionist. He constantly strove for high standards in his work and personal life. However, he felt that his perfectionism was causing him stress, anxiety and envy. He decided to give up perfectionism by recognising that perfection is an unattainable standard, and he does not need to prove his competence constantly through perfectionism. Pravin learnt to establish realistic expectations for himself as well as accept and embrace his flaws. He practiced self-compassion and self-care and learnt to celebrate his accomplishments, even though they may not meet his previous standards of perfection. Pravin found that by giving up perfectionism, he could enjoy the process of learning and growth, and his overall welfare and happiness improved.

Relinquishing control in parenting

Priyanka was struggling with the need to control every aspect of her children's lives as a parent. She was constantly worried about their security, performance in school and future success. However, she felt that her need for control was creating stress in her relationship with her children and preventing them from developing their autonomy and resilience. Priyanka decided to practice recognising how her children could learn through their experiences and lessons. She learnt to believe in her abilities and micromanage her life. Priyanka focused on creating a healthy as well as open relationship with her children based on trust, communication and mutual respect. She learnt to embrace the uncertainties of parenting as well as permitting her children to make mistakes and learn from them. After this, all her worries were over.

Letting go of negative ideas and beliefs

Sidharth had a constant flow of negative thoughts and self-doubt, which prevented him from pursuing his dreams and goals. He realised that these thoughts were not based on reality and prevented him from reaching his full potential. Sidharth decided to practice giving up negative thoughts and beliefs by becoming aware of them. He learnt to challenge their validity and change them with positive, empowered thoughts and beliefs. Sidharth practiced consciousness and self-compassion and learnt to give up those negative thoughts that were obstructing his progress. He sought help from a doctor as well and engaged in positive affirmations and self-dialogue. With time, Sidharth noticed a significant change in his intellect and overall welfare. He became more self-confident, flexible and optimistic.

Renunciation of material things

Leela felt that she had accumulated a lot of material possessions over the years, which were no longer useful to her. She decided to practice renunciation of material things by organising her house and simplifying her life. Leela sorted her stuff and kept only those things that actually gave her happiness and fulfilled a practical purpose. She donated or sold the rest of her possessions and learnt to separate her identity as well as worth from material possessions. Leela found that by giving up material possessions, there was room in her life for experiences, relationships and personal development. She also found that she did not need material possessions to define her happiness and that true satisfaction came from within.

Letting go of regret and guilt

Suresh had a heavy burden of regret and guilt over previous mistakes and failures on him. He found that he was constantly reflecting on events of the past and beating himself up for his perceived shortcomings. Suresh felt that regret and guilt were holding him in the past and preventing him from living fully in the present moment. He decided to practice letting go of regret and guilt by accepting his mistakes and failures without judgement and forgiving himself. Suresh also learnt to make improvements wherever possible and focus on the lessons learnt from his previous experiences, instead of living with regrets. He practiced self-compassion and self-forgiveness and adopted the intellect of growth and learning.

Letting go of comparison and judgement

Kishori often found herself comparing herself with others and assessing herself as well as others, based on external standards. She felt that this habit was making her feel not good enough, jealous and different from others. Kishori decided to practice letting go of comparison and judgement by creating an intellect of self-acceptance and non-judgement. She learnt to appreciate her unique qualities and strengths as well as accept differences in others without any judgement and celebrate them. Kishori practiced gratitude and consciousness by focusing on the current moment and blessings in her life. She actively prepared herself once again to make her thoughts and language more compassionate as well as accept herself and others. Kishori found that by giving up comparison and judgement, her self-respect, relationships and overall welfare have improved.

Finally, letting go is an art that requires practice, self-awareness and conscious effort. This is a process of giving up attachments, expectations and negative feelings that prevent us from living fully in the current moment. By mastering the art of letting go, we can liberate ourselves from the burden of the past, worries about the future and the limitations of our minds. We can develop acceptance, adaptability and intellectual flexibility as well as open ourselves to new possibilities, experiences and development. Letting go is not about accepting defeat or being passive; rather, it is about surrendering, in order to control and embrace the power of choice in the current moment.

Letting go is not always easy and can require conscious effort as well as practice. It can also include facing uncomfortable feelings as well as your own fears and insecurities. However, the benefits of letting go are immense. It permits us to give up our emotional burden which lightens us, makes room for new experiences and possibilities, and lets us live fully in the current moment.

❑

44

Managing Fear and Anxiety

Fear and anxiety are normal human emotions that can arise in different situations and impact our intellectual, emotional and physical health. From everyday stress to major life changes, fear and anxieties can sometimes make us feel burdened as well as obstruct our ability to live a full and balanced life. However, you may become a master of your own mind and manage fear and anxiety effectively. In this chapter, we shall explore strategies and examples to manage fear and anxiety, so that you can navigate challenging circumstances with flexibility and inner strength.

Understanding fear and anxiety

Fear and anxiety are natural responses to perceived dangers or dangers. They are part of our evolutionist survival strategy, which helps us counter possible loss and protect ourselves. Fear is a response to immediate danger, whereas, anxiety is often related to anticipated dangers or worries about future events.

Fear and worry may be helpful in some situations, such as when they inspire us to take necessary precautions or avoid risky behaviour, they can also burden us and interfere in our daily lives, if not managed effectively. Fear and anxiety can create different mental health issues in the long run, such as anxiety disorder, panic disorder, phobia and much more.

Examples of fear and anxiety-provoking situations can include:

Public speaking—Many people experience fear and anxiety while publicly speaking, whether before a large audience or participating in a meeting at work.

Financial stress—Anxiety about money, loans and financial instability can trigger worry and fear, which leads to stress and sleepless nights.

Health-related worries—Facing a serious ailment, undergoing a medical procedure, or worrying about the health of a loved one can become a cause for fear and anxiety.

Challenges of a relationship—Difficulties in relationships, such as conflict with a partner, family member or friend can trigger fear and anxiety.

Life changes—Major life changes, such as starting a new job, going to a new city, or going through a divorce can provoke fear and anxiety because we navigate unfamiliar territory.

Uncertainty—Facing unknown or unanticipated situations, such as economic change, political unrest, or global events can trigger fear and anxiety about the future.

Management of fear and anxiety

Although fear and anxiety are an indispensable part of the human experience, they can be managed effectively with the correct strategies and intellect. Some examples of techniques and perspectives are given here to help you manage fear and anxiety:

Practice self-awareness—The first step in the management of fear and anxiety is creating self-consciousness. When fear or anxiety arises, focus on your thoughts, feelings and physical sensations. Focus on any pattern, triggers or automatic negative thoughts that may be contributing to your fear and anxiety.

For example, if you observe that you catastrophise situations or hold negative thoughts about the future, then be conscious of these thoughts as well as challenge them with a more realistic and logical perspective. This can help you gain control over your thoughts and reduce the intensity of fear and anxiety.

Develop coping strategies—Developing coping strategies can help you manage fear and anxiety. Coping strategies are healthy ways of dealing with stress as well as emotions and can be different, based on the person. Examples of coping strategies include deep breathing exercises, practice of consciousness, exercise, journaling, talking to a trusted friend or doctor, and participating in hobbies or activities that give you happiness.

For example, if you feel anxious before public speaking, you can practice deep breathing to calm your nervous system, imagine yourself as being successful in the presentation, and fully prepare through practice and rehearsal. These coping strategies can help you manage the fear and anxiety related to public speaking.

Challenge negative thoughts—Fear and anxiety are often associated with negative thoughts which are included in the cycle of fear and anxiety. In order to be free of the hold of fear and anxiety, it is important to challenge these negative thoughts and beliefs. Ask yourself if your ideas are based on facts or beliefs. Are they rooted in reality or are they inspired by fear and anxiety? Is there any proof to support these ideas? Often, our fears and anxieties are based on illogical or exaggerated beliefs, which do not come under scrutiny.

For example, if you are worried about a job interview and have thoughts such as 'I am going to be unsuccessful' or 'I am not good enough', challenge them by asking yourself—Is there any solid evidence to support these beliefs? Are there any previous experiences or accomplishments that negate these negative thoughts? Change them with more balanced and logical ideas, such as 'I have prepared well for the interview and I will do my best' or 'I have the skills and abilities for this job'.

Practice awareness—Consciousness is a powerful tool to manage fear and anxiety. This includes focusing on the current moment without judgement and with full awareness. By practising consciousness, you can bring your focus to the here and now, instead of worrying about the future or regretting the past.

There are many such consciousness techniques that you can practice, such as meditation, body scan, and mindful breathing. When fear and anxiety arise, without trying to change it, you can bring your consciousness to your breathing, by focusing on the experience of inhaling and exhaling. This can help in calming your nervous system and bring you back to the present moment as well as reduce the intensity of fear and anxiety.

Create a support system—Having a support system can be invaluable in the management of fear and anxiety. Surround yourself with people who are sensible, neutral and helpful. Share your fears and anxieties with trusted friends, family members or doctors. Talking about your fears and anxieties can help you gain perspective, process your feelings, and obtain support as well as encouragement.

For example, if you are going through a challenging life transition, such as divorce or loss of job, having a helpful network of friends and family members can provide you with emotional support, practical help, and different perspectives on the situation. They can also remind you of your strengths and abilities which can increase your self-confidence and flexibility in managing fear and anxiety.

Practice self-care—Taking care of your physical, intellectual and emotional health is important for managing fear and anxiety. Ensure that you prioritise self-care in your routine. Get sufficient sleep, eat balanced meals, exercise regularly, and practice relaxation techniques such as yoga or meditation.

It is also important to take care of your intellectual and emotional health. Remain engaged in such activities that give you joy and satisfaction, practice self-compassion, and set healthy limits for the stress in your life. Taking overall care of yourself will help you create flexibility as well as manage fear and anxiety in a better way.

Challenge your comfort zone—Fear and anxiety are often created when we face new or unfamiliar circumstances. It can be scary to step out of our comfort zone but it can also be an opportunity for development and learning. By deliberately challenging your comfort zone, you can build flexibility and self-confidence in managing fear and anxiety.

For example, if you fear heights, you can slowly expose yourself to a height in a secure and controlled environment, such as climbing stairs or standing on the balcony of a tall building. You can rid yourself of the fear of heights through repeated performance and practice as well as develop more resilience in managing fear and anxiety in similar circumstances.

Practice acceptance—Acceptance is an important aspect of managing fear and anxiety. Acceptance does not mean letting go of fears and anxiety; rather, permitting yourself to accept their presence and experience them, without any judgement. Avoidance or resistance to fear and anxiety can often make them intense and increase their impact.

The practice of acceptance includes accepting your fears or anxiety without trying to change or suppress them. Let yourself feel those emotions that arise without judgement or self-criticism. Be kind and compassionate to yourself, while recognising that fear and anxiety are normal human emotions that everyone experiences, at one time or the other.

For example, if you are worried about any upcoming social event, practice acceptance by accepting your anxiety and permitting yourself to experience it fully, instead of eliminating it or avoiding it completely. You can say to yourself, "I feel worried about this event and it is alright. This is a normal human emotion and I can choose the option of participating in the programme, despite being worried."

Use visualisation techniques—Visualisation techniques can be a powerful instrument in managing fear and anxiety. When you are feeling scared or anxious, you can use your imagination to create positive intellectual images that counter negative thoughts and emotions.

For example, if you are worried about giving a presentation at work, you can close your eyes and imagine yourself giving a confident and successful presentation. Imagine yourself talking clearly with self-confidence, gaining a positive response from your audience, and feeling a sense of accomplishment. Visualisation techniques can help you build a positive intellect as well as reduce the intensity of fear and anxiety.

Seek professional help—It is important to seek professional help if fear and anxiety are significantly affecting your daily life and work. An able doctor or consultant can provide you with valuable tools, techniques and help in managing fear and anxiety.

Therapy can help you identify and explore the inherent causes of fear and anxiety, such as previous wounds or unresolved issues. This can also provide you with coping strategies, relaxation techniques, and cognitive interference in order to help you manage fear and anxiety in a healthy and effective way.

Finally, managing fear and anxiety is an important skill for controlling your own mind. This requires consciousness, self-compassion, and deliberate practice of different techniques and strategies. By challenging negative ideas, practising consciousness, creating a support system, practising self-care, challenging your comfort zone, practising acceptance, using visualisation techniques, and seeking professional help when required, you can gain flexibility and mastery over your fears and anxieties.

Remember that fear and anxiety are normal human emotions and it is fine to experience them. The key is to not let them control your life and prevent you from living fully. With practice and support, you can learn to manage fear and anxiety in a healthy and effective way. As a result, you can become a master of your own mind and live a more complete and empowered life.

❑

45

Enhancing Self-acceptance and Forgiveness

Self-acceptance and forgiveness are important factors of intellectual and emotional welfare. They permit us to develop a healthy relationship with ourselves, accept our flaws, and let go off self-blame and guilt. Self-acceptance and forgiveness are not about forgiving harmful behaviour; rather, they are about accepting our humanity, embracing self-compassion, and promoting inner healing and growth. In this chapter, we shall explore the importance of self-acceptance and forgiveness in our lives and how they can be enhanced in order to become masters of our own minds.

Results of lack of self-acceptance and forgiveness

When we lack self-acceptance and forgiveness, we can experience different negative results that can impact our intellectual and emotional welfare. These results can include:

Self-criticism and negative self-discussion—When we do not accept ourselves completely, we can engage in self-criticism and negative self-dialogue. We can curse ourselves constantly for our perceived flaws, mistakes and failures. This negative self-discussion can destroy our self-respect, create self-doubt, and contribute to a negative self-image.

Guilt and shame—Without forgiveness, we can take unresolved blame and shame from previous tasks or mistakes. We can reflect constantly on our previous failings and feel burdened with the weight of guilt and shame. This can create a perpetual cycle of self-punishment, inner destruction, and negative feelings.

Inner struggle and resistance—A lack of self-acceptance can create internal fighting and resistance within us. We can struggle to accept some aspects of our identity, beliefs or emotions, such as who are we? What do we think we should be? There can be an inner struggle between these questions. This can create internal stress and contribute to a sense of inner turmoil.

Stressful relationships—When we do not accept and forgive ourselves completely, it can affect our relationships with others. We can project our self-criticism, guilt or shame on others, which can cause tense relationships, lack of trust, and emotional distance.

Examples of promoting self-acceptance

Come, let us consider some examples of how we can increase self-acceptance in different aspects of our lives:

Body image—Neelam has been struggling with issues of body image for years. She has always compared herself with others, felt self-conscious about her looks, and criticised her body constantly. Neelam realises that her negative self-discussion and lack of self-acceptance are impacting her self-respect and overall well-being. She decides to practice self-acceptance by accepting her body without comparing it to others or criticising it and appreciating it. Neelam begins to focus on self-care and self-compassion and treats her body with kindness and respect. She practices positive affirmations, gratitude and consciousness in order to change her perspective and develop self-acceptance towards her body.

Past mistakes—Yogesh made a significant mistake at work which resulted in a financial loss to his company. He feels guilty and ashamed and curses himself constantly for his error. Yogesh realises that he cannot change the past and holding on to guilt and shame affects his intellectual health and productivity. He decides to practice self-acceptance by accepting his mistake, taking responsibility for it, and learning from it. He forgives himself for his mistake and is committed to learn and grow from the experience. Yogesh also seeks support from a trusted friend or adviser, who encourages him and helps him gain perspective on the situation. Yogesh lets go off the burden of guilt and shame through self-acceptance and forgiveness and moves forward with a feeling of peace and self-compassion.

Personal identity—Kamini is struggling to accept her sexual orientation. She has been hiding her true self from others and negating her own identity for fear of judgement and disapproval. Kamini realises that living falsely is causing her intellectual and emotional problems. She decides to practice self-acceptance by accepting her true self and being honest with herself and others. Kamini seeks help from a doctor who helps her explore her feelings, ideas and fears related to her sexual orientation. She educates herself about her identity, connects with others sharing similar experiences, and learns to embrace and accept herself completely. Through self-acceptance, Kamini is able to let go of the fear of judgement and live authentically, through which she feels a sense of liberation and inner peace.

Emotional vulnerability—Prakash has always struggled to express his feelings openly. He has adapted to thinking that showing vulnerability is a sign of weakness, and he has suppressed his feelings for most of his life. Prakash realises that his lack of self-acceptance and fear of being weak are affecting his relationships as well as his intellectual welfare. He decides to practice self-acceptance by accepting his feelings and respecting them, without judgement. Prakash begins to practice emotional intelligence by recognising his feelings, expressing them, and processing them in a healthy way. He learns to accept and honour his feelings as a natural part of being human and also communicates openly and authentically about his feelings with others.

Examples of increasing forgiveness

Come, let us consider some examples of how we can increase forgiveness in different aspects of our lives:

Forgiving others—Rakhi had a grudge against her friend who betrayed her trust. She realised that the anger and bitterness that she felt towards her friend were taking a toll on her intellectual and emotional health. Rakhi decided to practice forgiveness by accepting her feelings and making a conscious choice to let go of her resentment. She is engaged in self-reflection and sympathy and is trying to understand the reasons behind her friend's actions. Rakhi learnt to set healthy boundaries as well and communicated openly with her friend about how she felt. Through the practice of forgiveness, Rakhi could let go of negativity and move towards healing and reconciliation.

Forgiving yourself—Rakesh committed a mistake due to which his family faced an economic loss. He felt deeply guilty and ashamed and constantly punished himself emotionally for the error. Rakesh realised that he could not change the past and it was not right to hold on to guilt and shame. He decided to practice self-forgiveness by accepting his mistake, taking responsibility for it and learning from it. He granted compassion and understanding to himself, just as he would a loved one. Rakesh made amendments by taking steps to improve the situation and prevent these kinds of mistakes in the future as well. Through self-forgiveness, Rakesh was able to let go off the burden of guilt and shame. He moved towards self-healing and growth.

Forgiving life situations—Jessica experienced a traumatic event in her past that left her with deep emotional wounds. She is possessed by anger and frustration towards those circumstances that caused the shock. Jessica realised that holding on to anger and frustration was not serving her well and was preventing her from moving forward in her life. She decided to practice forgiveness for those life circumstances that she could not change. Jessica connected with medicine and other healing methods in order to process her feelings and gain perspective on the situation. She learnt to accept the past and focus on her present and future. Through forgiveness, Jessica could give up her emotional state and build a more positive and full life.

Forgiving unresolved relationships—Mohan had a tense relationship with his father due to misunderstandings and mistakes of the past. He had malice and a grudge towards his father which created tension in their relationship and affected Mohan's intellectual and emotional welfare as well. Mohan realised that holding on to the past and resentment was not providing him with any peace or resolution. He decided to practice forgiveness by going to his father and initiating an open and honest dialogue. Mohan expressed his feelings and listened to his father's viewpoint, without judgement. He learnt to let go off the need to be right and instead, focus on understanding and exploring common facts.

Finally, increasing self-acceptance and forgiveness are essential aspects of gaining control over our minds. Through self-acceptance, we learn to embrace and love ourselves unconditionally, with all our strengths and weaknesses. We learn to accept our feelings, thoughts and experiences without any judgement and develop a positive relationship with ourselves. Self-acceptance permits us to let go of self-doubt, self-criticism and the need for external validation, and enables us to live an authentic and full life.

On the other hand, forgiveness liberates us from the emotional burden of the sorrows, regrets and frustration of the past. It permits us to let go off negativity, promote healing, and move towards reconciliation and resolution. Forgiveness is not about forgiving or forgetting the actions of others or ourselves; rather, it is about letting go off the emotional attachment to the pain and wounds associated with those actions. It is a conscious choice to liberate oneself from the past as well as build a more positive and empowered present and future.

❑

46

Enhancing Self-confidence

Self-confidence is an important aspect of our intellectual welfare and overall success in life. It is the foundation of a positive self-image, strong self-respect, and confidence in our own abilities. When we believe in ourselves, we are more likely to pursue our goals, face challenges with resilience, and achieve our full potential. However, many people struggle with self-confidence and often experience self-doubt, fear of failure, and lack of confidence in their abilities. The good news is that self-confidence is a skill that can be developed and enhanced through practice and consciousness. In this chapter, we shall explore strategies and examples of how to increase self-confidence and become masters of our own minds.

Understanding self-confidence

Self-confidence is confidence in one's value, abilities and strength. It is not about being arrogant or proud; rather, it is about having a realistic and positive perception of yourself. Self-confidence is an inner state of the mind that shows our thoughts, feelings and behaviour towards ourselves. It is affected by different factors including our upbringing, experiences and environment. However, self-confidence is neither steady nor neutral but is a dynamic quality that can be developed and strengthened with time.

Increasing self-confidence

Recognise and challenge limiting beliefs—One of the first steps in increasing self-confidence is to identify any limiting beliefs and challenge them that can hold you back. Limiting beliefs are negative ideas or beliefs about yourself that create self-doubt and weaken your self-confidence. For example, thoughts like 'I am not good enough', 'I am unsuccessful', or 'I will never be successful' are limiting beliefs that can negatively impact your self-confidence.

In order to challenge limiting beliefs, start by being aware of them. Pay attention to when these negative thoughts arise and question their validity. Ask yourself if there is any proof to support these beliefs and whether they are based on any facts or assumptions. Challenge these beliefs with more logical and positive ideas. For example, if you find yourself thinking, "I am not good enough", change it with a more empowered thought, like "I am able and worthy of success."

Example—Kalpana is a young professional who struggles with self-confidence at work. She often feels inferior to her colleagues and doubts her abilities to face new challenges. Through self-reflection, she realises that she is limiting her beliefs about her abilities, such as 'I am not smart enough' and 'I am not experienced enough'. She challenges these beliefs by evaluating her previous successes and accepting her strengths and skills. She changes her limiting beliefs with more positive and logical ideas, such as 'I have proved my abilities in the past and I am capable of learning and growing in my role'. This change in her intellect increases her self-confidence and permits her to take on new responsibilities at work with a more positive outlook.

Set realistic goals and achieve them—Another effective way of increasing self-confidence is to set realistic goals and work in the direction of achieving them. When we set attainable goals and take steps in the direction of achieving them, we experience a feeling of accomplishment and satisfaction which can increase our self-confidence.

Start by setting specific, measurable and attainable goals that align with your values and interests. Divide them into small, manageable steps and prepare a plan to achieve them. Celebrate your progress along the way and accept your accomplishments, however small they may appear to be. This will help you create a sense of self-efficacy and self-confidence in your abilities.

Example—Kamal is a college student who wants to improve his self-confidence in public speaking. He aims to give a presentation before his class by the end of the semester. He divides the goal into small stages, such as researching the subject, preparing the outline, practising in front of the mirror, and giving the presentation to a small group of friends for feedback. He follows his plan diligently and accepts his progress at each stage. Finally, he gives the presentation to his class and gains positive feedback. This accomplishment increases his self-confidence in public speaking and encourages him to take up more opportunities to speak in the future.

Embrace failure as an opportunity to learn—Fear of failure is a common obstacle in the way of self-confidence. Many people avoid taking risks or pursuing their goals because they are scared of failing and facing disapproval or disappointment. However, failure is a natural part of life and can be a valuable opportunity for learning that can, in fact, increase self-confidence.

Instead of being scared of failure, adopt it as an opportunity for learning, growth and improvement. Change your intellect of viewing failure as a reflection of your abilities with a reaction that can help you refine your approach and make better choices in the future. Adopt an intellect of development that is focused on constant improvement instead of perfection.

Example—Janki is an ambitious entrepreneur who dreams of starting her own business. However, she fears failure and hesitates to take the first step. Through self-reflection, she realises that the fear of failure is preventing her from pursuing her passion. She changes her intellect and begins to view failure as an opportunity of learning, instead of a reflection of her self-worth. She takes small steps towards her goal, such as doing market research, preparing a business plan, and reaching out to mentors for guidance. She has to face challenges and failures along the way, but she learns from them and continues to move forward. Her self-confidence increases slowly because she realises that failure is a step towards success.

Practice self-compassion—Self-compassion is the practice of behaving with kindness, understanding and acceptance with yourself, especially during difficult times or while facing challenges. It involves being helpful and nurturing towards yourself, just as anyone would be with a friend or loved one. The practice of self-compassion can increase self-confidence by reducing self-criticism, self-judgement, and negative self-dialogue.

While facing failures or challenges, practice self-compassion instead of cursing yourself or holding on to self-critical thoughts. Treat yourself with kindness, accept your feelings, and offer words of encouragement to yourself. Remind yourself that everyone makes mistakes and faces challenges and it is fine(okay) not to be perfect. Embrace self-acceptance and forgive yourself for any perceived shortcomings or failures.

Example—Manohar is a professional athlete who has recently experienced a shock (jolt) in his performance. He feels disappointed and frustrated and his self-confidence wavers. Instead of focusing on self-criticism and negative self-dialogue, he practices self-compassion. He accepts his feelings and provides himself with words of comfort and encouragement. He reminds himself that failures are a part of the journey of success and he is not alone in facing challenges. He treats himself kindly and provides himself with the same level of support and understanding as he would a team member. This self-compassionate approach helps him to bounce back from the shock and rebuild his self-confidence.

Surround yourself with positive and helpful people—The people with whom we surround ourselves can have a significant impact on our self-confidence. Negative or unhelpful people can bring us down and destroy our self-confidence, whereas, positive and helpful people can uplift us and increase our self-confidence.

Choose to spend time with those people who believe in you, support your goals, and provide positive feedback and encouragement. Surround yourself with those people who inspire you, challenge you to grow, and celebrate your successes. Do not expose yourself to negative influences or disparate relationships, which bring you down or reduce your self-confidence.

Example—Emily is a young professional who has recently started a new job in a competitive industry. She comes to know that some of her colleagues are criticising her work constantly and making negative comments about her abilities. This begins to affect her self-confidence and she starts to doubt her abilities. However, she adopts a proactive approach and seeks out positive and helpful people at her workplace. She befriends those colleagues who believe in her as well as provide creative feedback and encouragement. She takes advice from senior colleagues as well, who inspire her and provide guidance. Surrounding herself with positive and helpful people helps her regain her self-confidence and perform better in her job.

Set attainable goals and celebrate your progress—Setting attainable goals and celebrating your progress can increase self-confidence. When you set realistic goals and work in the direction of achieving them, you create a sense of purpose, direction and accomplishment. By celebrating your progress along the way, you accept your efforts and strengthen positive behaviour, which can increase your self-confidence.

Take care of your physical and intellectual health—Our physical and intellectual health is closely linked to our self-confidence. When we take care of our body and mind, we feel better about ourselves. This can increase our self-confidence.

Focus on your physical health by eating balanced meals, exercising regularly, and getting sufficient sleep. Exercise has been shown to improve mood, reduce stress, and increase self-respect. It is equally important to take care of our intellectual health as well. Practice self-care activities, such as meditation and relaxation techniques. Seek help from a therapist or counsellor if required and participate in such activities that provide you happiness and satisfaction.

Challenge negative ideas and beliefs—Negative ideas and beliefs can have an important effect on our self-confidence. Often, we have limiting beliefs about ourselves that hold us back and prevent us from reaching our full potential. Challenging these negative ideas and beliefs can help us gain a more realistic and positive perspective, which can increase our self-confidence.

Be aware of any negative thoughts or beliefs arising in your mind and question their validity. Ask yourself whether they are based on facts or perceptions. Challenge negative ideas by providing evidence to the contrary and reframe them in a more positive light. Change negative self-dialogue with positive as well as empowering statements. Practice positive self-discussion and develop an intellect of self-encouragement and self-compassion.

Embrace failure as an opportunity for learning—Failure is a natural part of life and everyone experiences failure at some point or the other. However, how we feel and react to failure can majorly influence our self-confidence. Embracing failure as an opportunity for learning can help us develop flexibility, learn from our mistakes, and eventually, increase our self-confidence.

Instead of seeing failure as a reflection of your competence or abilities, view it as an opportunity to learn and grow. Reflect on what went wrong. What could you have done differently and what can you learn from the experience? Use failure as a stepping stone to improvement and success. Remember that even the most successful people have experienced failure and this does not define their worth or abilities.

Step out of your comfort zone—Stepping out of your comfort zone and facing new challenges can greatly increase your self-confidence. When you challenge yourself and move out of your comfort zone, you prove to yourself that you are capable of achieving those things about which you had never even thought. This can increase your self-confidence and expand your abilities.

Identify those areas of your life where you remain inside your comfort zone and make a conscious effort to step out of it. Set such goals which require you to expand yourself and take calculated risks. Embrace new experiences, try new things, and remain open to learning and development. Keep in mind that progress and development lie outside your comfort zone, and taking risks can lead to increased new opportunities and self-confidence.

Finally, self-confidence is an important factor in gaining success and perfection in life. It is not natural, rather it is a skill that can be developed and increased through deliberate effort and practice. We can increase our self-confidence by applying the strategies discussed in this chapter, such as changing our intellect, skill building, seeking support, setting goals, practising self-compassion, embracing failure as an opportunity of learning, and stepping outside our comfort zone, as well as become masters of our self-confidence and our mind.

Remember that enhancing self-confidence is a continuous process that requires patience, determination and self-consciousness. It is normal to encounter moments of self-doubt and failures along the way, but with constant efforts and positive intellect, we can overcome these obstacles and create a strong foundation of self-confidence. By believing in ourselves, recognising our strengths, learning from our mistakes and challenging negative thoughts, we can unlock our full potential and achieve our goals with self-confidence.

So, take your first step today in the direction of increasing your self-confidence. Reflect on the strategies discussed in this chapter and identify those areas in your life where you can apply them. Surround yourself with helpful people, set realistic goals, and treat yourself with compassion. With dedication and practice, you can use your mind fruitfully as well as increase your self-confidence to new heights and pave the way for a successful and fulfilling life. Remember, you are capable of achieving greatness and your self-confidence is the key to unlocking your full potential. Believe in yourself, take action and watch your self-confidence soar!

❑

Conclusion

As you come to the end of this book, *Student Mind Power,* I hope that you have gained valuable insight and tools to help you in your journey towards self-mastery. We have explored the various aspects of the mind in all the chapters, which include self-consciousness, consciousness, emotional management, communication, and self-confidence. We have explored practical strategies, examples and exercises that can empower you to control your mind and create a life that aligns with your true self.

We have stressed the importance of self-consciousness as the basis of self-mastery in the entire book. By being more conscious of your thoughts, feelings and beliefs, you can gain clarity about your inner perspective and understand how it affects your actions and behaviours. Self-consciousness permits you to recognise patterns, triggers and habitual responses which do not serve you well. It empowers you to make conscious choices in the current moment.

We have also explored the power of meditation, which involves focusing on the current moment without judgement. Consciousness enables you to develop a non-reactive, compassionate and curious attitude towards your ideas and feelings and empowers you to answer them swiftly. By practising consciousness, you can develop more emotional regulation, reduce stress and anxiety as well as enhance your overall well-being.

Apart from this, we have discussed the importance of managing negative emotions and developing healthy communication skills. You can get help in navigating challenging situations with grace and flexibility by learning to manage negative emotions as anger, fear and sadness. Healthy communication skills, such as listening actively, expressing yourself vocally, and resolving conflicts with sympathy and understanding, can improve your relationships, both personally as well as professionally.

Apart from this, we have explored the role of self-confidence in self-mastery. Creating self-confidence includes developing a positive self-image, challenging self-limiting beliefs, setting realistic goals, and taking consistent action in the direction of achieving them. Building self-confidence is a process that requires practice, determination as well as self-compassion, and it can greatly affect your ability to pursue your dreams and live a fulfilling life.

We have also stressed the importance of self-care, forgiveness and self-acceptance in nurturing a positive intellect and building flexibility, in this entire book. It is important to take care of your physical, intellectual and emotional health in order to maintain a healthy and balanced mind. Forgiveness, both for yourself and others, permits healing as well as liberation from the burden of complaints and dissatisfaction. Self-acceptance involves including all aspects of yourself, which includes your flaws as well as mistakes, and loving yourself unconditionally.

As you consider the teachings and exercises shared in this book, it is important to remember that self-mastery is a lifelong journey. It is not about achieving perfection or eliminating all challenges from your life. It is about developing self-consciousness, consciousness and the practice of ongoing deliberate action. It is about constantly learning, growing and developing as a person.

You may have to face failures, obstacles and moments of doubt on your journey towards self-mastery. It is important to remember that it is a part of the process and it is fine to make mistakes and experience failures. What is important is how you respond to these challenges. By applying the tools and strategies shared in this book, you can navigate difficult times with flexibility, knowledge and grace.

It is also important to accept that self-mastery is a personal journey and every person's path can be different. What works for one person may not work for another and that is fine. It is important to find out what resonates with you as well as prepare methods and techniques according to your specific requirements and circumstances. Believe in yourself and your inner knowledge because you are on your way to self-mastery.

As you finish your reading of this book, I encourage you to take action as well as apply the teachings and methods in your daily life. Keep in mind that change takes time and effort and progress cannot always be linear. Be patient with yourself and celebrate your successes, however small they may seem to be.

Apart from this, surround yourself with a helpful group of people with similar ideologies, who can encourage and uplift you in your journey towards self-mastery. Search for advisers, trainers or friends who can provide guidance, accountability and encouragement, so that you can gain mastery of your own mind by navigating challenges and victories (because you navigate your own mind among the challenges and victories of gaining mastery).

When you move forward on your path towards self-mastery, keep in mind that it is a continuous process. Like physical health, intellectual as well as emotional health requires constant care and attention. Prioritise self-care in your life and regularly assess as well as reassess your thoughts, emotions and behaviours so that it can be ensured that they are relevant to your values and goals.

Keep in mind that self-mastery is not about perfectionism; rather, it is about progress. Embrace your flaws, learn from your mistakes, and use them as opportunities for development and self-improvement. Be kind and benevolent towards yourself and practice self-acceptance as well as forgiveness, while navigating the ups and downs of life.

When you continue your journey towards self-mastery, always remember to be true to yourself. Listen to the voice of your conscience, trust your intuition, and remain true to your values and beliefs. Avoid comparing yourself to others or seeking external validation and instead, focus on your progress and development. Embrace your specialty and celebrate your individuality.

Finally, I hope that this book has provided you with valuable insight, strategies and tools, that will help you become a master of your own mind. Keep in mind that self-mastery is a continuous journey and requires constant practice, self-consciousness, and deliberate action. Accept challenges, celebrate successes, and always try to be the best version of yourself.

I feel honoured to accompany you on this journey, and I wish you all the best in your search for self-mastery. As you continue to develop your intellect and build a life aligned with your deep desires and aspirations, you can find inner peace, stability and satisfaction.

❑